Rationality Is...
The Essence of
Literary Theory

Dear Al + Lee

It's a pleasure getting to know you better and better. I do think this book could help a lot of people with whom you have regular contact or who sit in the pews who have had experience of a challenging (confusing) education (especially) arts subjects over the years. I hope you find it useful.

With love,
M

Rationality Is . . .
The **Essence** of Literary Theory

—— Norm Klassen ——

CASCADE *Books* • Eugene, Oregon

RATIONALITY IS . . . THE ESSENCE OF LITERARY THEORY

Copyright © 2022 Norm Klassen. All rights reserved. Except for brief quotations in critical publications or reviews, no part of this book may be reproduced in any manner without prior written permission from the publisher. Write: Permissions, Wipf and Stock Publishers, 199 W. 8th Ave., Suite 3, Eugene, OR 97401.

Cascade Books
An Imprint of Wipf and Stock Publishers
199 W. 8th Ave., Suite 3
Eugene, OR 97401

www.wipfandstock.com

PAPERBACK ISBN: 978-1-6667-3018-0
HARDCOVER ISBN: 978-1-6667-2134-8
EBOOK ISBN: 978-1-6667-2135-5

Cataloguing-in-Publication data:

Names: Klassen, Norm [author.]

Title: Rationality is . . . the essence of literary theory / by Norm Klassen.

Description: Eugene, OR: Cascade Books, 2022 | Includes bibliographical references and index.

Identifiers: ISBN 978-1-6667-3018-0 (paperback) | ISBN 978-1-6667-2134-8 (hardcover) | ISBN 978-1-6667-2135-5 (ebook)

Subjects: LCSH: Literature—Philosophy | Literature—Theory, etc.—History and criticism | Literature—History and criticism—Theory, etc. | Criticism, interpretation, etc. | Criticism | Reason

Classification: PN94 K53 2022 (print) | PN94 (ebook)

05/25/22

Excerpts from "The Outlaw" from OPENED GROUND: SELECTED POEMS 1996–1996 by Seamus Heaney. Copyright © 1998 by Seamus Heaney. Reprinted by permission of Farrar, Straus and Giroux and Faber and Faber. All Rights Reserved.

"The Outlaw" from DOOR INTO THE DARK by Seamus Heaney. Copyright © 1969 by Seamus Heaney. Reprinted by permission of Farrar, Straus and Giroux, LLC and Faber and Faber.

Thanks to Daniel Kumin for permission to quote "Woodchucks" from OUR GROUND TIME HERE WILL BE BRIEF by Maxine Kumin. Copyright © 1972.

"Sex Without Love" from THE DEAD & THE LIVING by Sharon Olds, copyright ©1975, 1978, 1979, 1980, 1981, 1982, 1983 by Sharon Olds. Used by permission of Alfred A. Knopf, an imprint of the Knopf Doubleday Publishing Group, a division of Penguin Random House LLC. All rights reserved.

Thanks to Joan Eichner and Elke Inkster for permission to quote "The Hid, Here." Reprinted from ALWAYS NOW (in three volumes) by Margaret Avison by permission of the Porcupine's Quill. Copyright © The Estate of Margaret Avison, 2003.

Doctor and Doll by Norman Rockwell. Printed by permission of the Norman Rockwell Family Agency. Copyright © 1929 the Norman Rockwell Family Entities. Illustration provided by Curtis Licensing.

The Plays of William Shakespeare image in puzzle form. Image by Simon Drew, copyright © Simon Drew, 1996. Puzzle by Robert Longstaff, copyright © Robert Longstaff, 1996. Thanks to both for permission.

Modern quotations of the Bible are from the New Revised Standard Version Bible, copyright 1989, Division of Christian Education of the National Council of the Churches of Christ in the United States of America. Used by permission. All rights reserved.

For my students, for students everywhere.

"Eestward I beheld aftir the sonne
And say a tour—as I trowed, Treuthe was there-ynne;
Westward I waytede in a while aftir
And seigh a depe dale—Deth, as I leve,
Woned in tho wones, and wikkede spirites.
A fair feld ful of folk fond I ther bytwene
Of alle manere men, the mene and the riche,
Worchyng and wandryng as this world asketh."

Eastward I looked in the direction of the sun
And saw a tower—I thought, Truth was in there;
After a while I looked westward
And saw a deep dale—death, so I believe,
Lived in those parts, and wicked spirits.
I found a fair field full of folk in between
Of all manner of people, the poor and the rich,
Working and wandering as this world demands.

—William Langland, *The Vision of Piers Plowman*

Contents

List of Illustrations | xii
Preface | xiii
Acknowledgements | xv

Introduction | 1
   One Idea 1
   The Emperor's New Clothes? 3
   Theory and Contemporary Society 4
   Rationality, Theory, and Language 5
   Not the Last Word 7

The Critique of Rationality in Literature and Theory

1. The Critique of Rationality in Literature | 13
   Introduction 13
   Advice about Poetry 13
   The Critique of Rationality in Three Poems 16
   Conclusion 21

2. Rationality Is Male | 23
   Introduction 23
   Feminism 24
   Mimicry and Masculine Logic 27
   The Stupid Suburban Wife in "Bluebeard's Egg" 30
   Conclusion 33

CONTENTS

3. Rationality Is White | 34

　Introduction　34

　Critical Race Theory　35

　Heterogeneity and Hegemonic Thinking　38

　Generations and Heterogeneity in "Two Kinds"　43

　Conclusion　44

4. Rationality Is Repression | 45

　Introduction　45

　Freudian Psychoanalysis　47

　The Irrationality of the Uncanny　52

　Rationality and Repression in "The Use of Force"　56

　Conclusion　59

5. Conclusion to Section I | 60

False Problems: Towards the Recovery of Rationality

6. Introduction to Section II | 65

7. Rationality Is Judgement | 68

　Introduction　68

　Reason and Emotion, Facts and Values　69

　Before Alienation and Judgement　74

　Conclusion　80

8. Rationality Is Verification | 81

　Introduction　81

　Hermeneutics and Poetics　82

　Poetry, Textuality, and the Actuality That Is There　87

　Poetic Participation　89

　Conclusion　95

Language and the Critique of Rationality

9. Introduction to Section III | 99
   Language and the Rise of Theory   99
   The Prevailing Scientific and Common-Sense View of Language   101

10. Rationality Is Logocentric | 103
    Introduction   103
    A Philosophical Source of Post-Structuralism   104
    Saussure and Structuralism   107
    Saussure on the Sign, Arbitrariness, and Difference   109
    Derridean Deconstruction   113
    Derrida and the Tomb of Language   117
    Conclusion   119

11. Rationality Is Real | 120
    Introduction   120
    Lacan, I'm Your Father   121
    Lacan's Unconscious and Saussure's Signifying Chain   123
    Rationality as Procrustean Bed in "The Purloined Letter"   128
    Conclusion   131

12. Rationality Is Unities | 132
    Introduction   132
    A Question of Method   133
    History and the Suspension of Unities   135
    Culture, Context, and Co-texts   138
    The Limits of Control in "Babylon Revisited"   140
    Conclusion   142

Conclusion | 144
   Of Emperors and Little Boys   144
   Post-Critical Hope   146

Bibliography | 149
Index | 153

List of Illustrations

Timeline: The development of theory in the 1960s | 25

Generations | 41

Generations and heterogeneity | 41

Timeline: The seventeenth century to the twentieth century | 47

Timeline: Classical civilizations and Christianity | 48

Timeline: Schism, Reformation, and first philosophy | 48

Timeline: Overview of Western eras | 49

Doctor and Doll (1929) by Norman Rockwell | 56

Timeline: The seventeenth century to the twentieth century | 78

Timeline: The Enlightenment, Nietzsche, Saussure, Derrida | 104

Timeline: Saussure, structuralism, and Saussure's spreading influence | 109

Timeline: The pre-Socratics in context | 116

Timeline: Saussure, structuralism, and Saussure's spreading influence | 122

"The Plays of William Shakespeare" rebus | 125

Figure and ground images | 126

Preface

This book offers an introduction to literary theory for students of literature, those in any arts or social science discipline, and general readers. A sub-discipline within literary studies, literary theory has developed in parallel form in other arts and social science disciplines, so that one might refer to "cultural theory" or "social theory" as well, or even just to "theory." For years, departments have integrated it into their programs. In short, this book treats "theory" as a significant but not always well-understood aspect of many people's undergraduate education and as an influence on culture. It's as familiar as the word "postmodern" and as tricky as "deconstruction." What's it about? What's at stake?

At a very basic level, theory concerns rationality. The title encourages two different interpretations of what it might mean to say so. On the one hand, the phrase *Rationality Is . . .* can be completed in any number of ways that suggest that what passes for rationality is best described in other terms. Mainstream theory takes this view. For instance, for feminism, what goes by the name amounts to male bias asserting itself from a position of power. Rationality is *male*. For critical race theory, the concept reinforces the position of a historically dominant group in north Atlantic societies. Rationality is *white*. Such phrases imply heavy irony and a very dim view of the Western philosophical tradition, especially after Plato. On this understanding, the essence of literary theory is the unmasking and redescription of rationality in other terms.

I believe that many people, upon first encountering it, understand well enough theory's critique and are justifiably uncomfortable with its implications. I suspect many come to interpret their misgivings as their own confusion or misunderstanding. This book encourages their acceptance of the substance of mainstream theory's critique, but not its abandonment of rationality in the Western tradition.

One can also read the book's title in a second way, as though the ellipsis indicates merely a pause before the completion of a thought. On this reading, *rationality itself is the essence of literary theory*. Along these lines, one might observe that the critique of rationality nevertheless indicates an obsession with it: the critic stands in a tradition. Still further, to say that it is the essence of literary theory affirms rationality as central to literature, to art, and to society. Certain conceptions of what it entails are indeed problematic, incomplete, and prideful. Scientific detachment, bureaucratization, and a bourgeois economic outlook all fail to do justice to rationality's true nature, which entwines with mystery. *The critique in the first way of reading the title remains relevant.* Yet one can still affirm rationality as integral to human flourishing, including the processes of producing, analyzing, and enjoying literature and art.

For the benefit of the lover of literature perhaps skeptical of theory's relevance, one might observe that the critique of rationality appears in literature itself. Lovers of poetry and fiction may rightly feel that they already recognize, at least tacitly, theory's central concern. Literature invites one to question what passes for order, sense, objectivity, the settled view of things. Theory does not come to literature entirely from the outside; in many ways it develops from within.

Yet literary theory does come from the outside too: from philosophy, from linguistics, from history, and from other disciplines. It involves foreign-sounding isms, each with its own terminology and representative voices that can make theory daunting. It remains indispensable nonetheless. Theory demands reflection on one's most basic guiding assumptions. It has had a profound impact on the humanities and social sciences, and on the wider culture as well, even as literature and culture have in their turn helped to shape its development.

If this book affirms the place of rationality in literature, art, and theory alike, it stops well short of embracing rationalism. Rationality alone neither fulfils nor explains the deepest longing of the human heart. Our dignity manifests itself as reason opening onto transcendent mystery, which accompanies its very operations. Paradoxically, rationality suggests itself to be already a response to and sign of fittedness for something more. It heightens our sensitivity to the reality of this moreness, and it urges hope.

Norm Klassen
25 April 2022

Acknowledgements

My thoughts about how this book came to be run to the many students to whom I have taught introductory literary theory over the years, to their questions, their objections, their requests for clarification, their insights, their aha! moments, and especially their occasional expressions of deep satisfaction with the way theory has made them more intellectually aware and, even more, helped them appreciate literature and their undergraduate calling in a new way. Certain names and faces have simply stuck with me, including: DeVonne Friesen, Dragica Stanivuk, Calla Churchward, Mike Turman, Emily Corner, Derek Lindman, Philip Cutmore, Ralph Neill, Cosmin Dzsurdzsa, Todd Anderson, Emily Fraser, Adan Jerreat-Poole, Lillian Wheeler, Kathleen Slofstra, Chantal Desereville, Max Kennel, Natalie Dewan, Yuriy Blokhin, Rafe Fernandes, Alejandra Alfaro Algumedo, Matt Bushey, Taylor Hatkoski, Alex Palczewski, Ken Ruffolo, Pam Schmidt, Nem Simic, Yomatie Persaud, Aarjan Giri, Anna Good, Masha Janjuz, Heather Stonehouse, Alex Perry, Julia Baker, David Brown, Claudia George, Vienna Hall, Kenny Hoang, Rachel Zehr, Ben Schwartzentruber, Hillary Ho, Youssef Hassan, Uriel Kogut, Amira Taneja, Ammaarah Shiraz, Sonia Laposi, Omar El Refai, Patricia Fagan, Nicole Riddle, Michael Clubine. Special thanks to those who read some version of the manuscript of this book, including Andrew and Maya Clubine, Eric Wallace, and Matt Sleiman, or have otherwise been especially supportive of this project, including Mae Fernandes.

    I would like also to thank the whole gang at Wipf and Stock, and especially my learned and encouraging editor Robin Parry.

Introduction

One Idea

Canadian scientist and public intellectual David Suzuki has commented on a shortcoming in scientific thinking. He challenges a way of approaching reality that in some ways provides the model for what counts as rationality in contemporary societies:

> Most of modern science, especially in the life sciences, is based on reductionism, which is focusing on a part of nature. We try to bring that fragment—a sub-atomic particle, atom, molecule, cell, etc.—into the lab where we can control, manipulate and measure it. . . . But in the process of focusing on a part, we remove it from the context within which it exists and interacts and so we are blind to the rhythms, patterns and cycles that impinge on it.[1]

Focusing on a part has brought many benefits, but the scientific method makes us "blind" to "rhythms, patterns and cycles." There are limitations to the scientific desire to "control, manipulate and measure," implicitly moral as well as rational ones.

Economics, as a social science, also contributes to the model of what it looks like to think rationally. Suzuki makes the case for humility in this discipline as well: "we have to openly acknowledge the strengths and weaknesses of both the scientific enterprise and the economic system that shapes so much of our lives."[2] In the modern period, science and economic thought have permeated most aspects of ordinary life. They have in many ways come to provide the template for what counts as knowable or rational.

---

1. Suzuki, "Environmentalism," 8.
2. Suzuki, "Environmentalism," 8.

INTRODUCTION

Yet they have weaknesses as well as strengths. They need to be approached with a recognition of their inherent limitations.

Suzuki offers a wise if quite preliminary critique of some of the assumptions of scientific-economic thought. Various observers and movements have, especially in the past one hundred years, put pressure on the notion of "rationality" itself. Their critiques encompass even more than science and economics, dominant though these are in the modern imagination. For instance, one important line of inquiry has involved a reconsideration of how language works, what it is for, and what it suggests about being human. Literary theory has developed out of some of these changes.

Literature itself has always asked awkward questions about what counts as obvious, as clear thinking, as the way things must be. It perennially invites reflection on the nature of rationality. Its questions challenge tyrannies and bureaucracies, overconfidence and dulled senses. Under the pressure of twentieth-century developments in philosophy, linguistics, and other disciplines, this interrogation has intensified in the form of literary theory. While theory does many different things and takes many different forms, one central concern preoccupies it: the status of rationality itself. This book offers an introduction to literary theory through the lens of this concern.

In mainstream theory, what passes for rationality is perceived to be a mask for something else that is going on. An influential theory textbook, one that will serve as an ongoing conversation partner, identifies a "cultural error of taking the dominant for the universal."[3] The Western philosophical tradition associates the notion of the universal with the work of rationality. In a landmark development, the whole of that tradition has been called into question:

> As a result of this argument, *all the values of the metaphysical tradition had to be put in question* because they all assumed the primacy and the priority of presence, substance, and identity as foundations while nonetheless describing the fact that difference, something insubstantial and nonpresent, made them possible.[4]

and . . .

---

3. Rivkin and Ryan, *Literary Theory* 3, 893. (See the bibliography for a note on source citations.)

4. Rivkin and Ryan, *Literary Theory* 2, 261 (emphasis mine).

> Post-Structuralists claim all such orders [imposed by rationality in the Western philosophical tradition] are strategies of power and social control, ways of ignoring reality rather than understanding it.[5]

If theory—understood in these terms—is right, then rationality and the Western metaphysical tradition that carries it are inherently problematic. If theory expresses the beating heart of literature and of art, then these disciplines or practices also must be skeptical about rationality and proceed by other means. Do they? Do we want to assume that they do?

The Emperor's New Clothes?

Becoming acquainted with literary theory is a little like sitting at the grown-ups' table and a little like the story about the emperor's new clothes. Sitting at the grown-ups' table is a transitional experience in a young person's life, one full of excitement and other, conflicting emotions. Everyone has their own tale to tell about it. The story about the emperor's new clothes, meanwhile, is about an emperor who is beguiled into thinking that he is wearing clothes that are invisible to the unintelligent when in fact he is simply naked. When he processes before the townsfolk, no one dares to say anything because they do not want to appear stupid, until a small boy states the obvious.

A relatively recent development and now integral aspect of the study of literature, literary theory is very exciting, necessary, and important. Becoming acquainted with it can make one feel grown up. Theory's critique of rationality, however, poses a problem. If rationality can always be revealed to be hiding something else, such as the interests of a gender or a racial group, then does rationality even exist as a meaningful category? If it does not, then how can one even talk about it? How does one conduct a debate? What are one's points of reference?

These are not trivial questions, and they are not posed here to invite glib answers. Nonetheless, one might have the nagging sensation of being in the presence of the emperor wearing his new clothes. One might have the sense, that is, of there being something wrong with a situation in which rationality itself is being *interrogated*. In the story, no one wants to say anything for fear of being humiliated. Doubts persist, confusion mounts.

---

5. Rivkin and Ryan, *Literary Theory* 3, 446.

INTRODUCTION

At this point, though, the analogy reaches its limits. Literary theory *is* important, it is not simply a deception. There is no little boy to dispel it as an illusion. "Rationality" as a concept one thinks one understands needs to be challenged. Scientific thinking and objective description, for example, do not, in and of themselves, adequately model what qualifies as rationality. They are incomplete.

Yet whereas mainstream theory encourages one to abandon the Western philosophical tradition that has nurtured a commitment to rationality, this book ultimately defends that tradition. Rationality belongs at the center of literary theory, *as it belongs at the heart of literature and the arts, politics and society*. In the context of contemporary assumptions about literary or cultural theory, it is right to think that there is an obviousness to the situation, as in the story of the emperor's new clothes. One is confronted with a decision. Literature and literary theory invite deep questions about what one thinks rationality entails. One will have to decide for oneself whether the tradition that nurtures it ought itself to be upheld.

Theory and Contemporary Society

What would our cultural situation look like if broad swathes of students who encountered theory, as many do, carried a certain confusion with them into William Langland's "fair field full of folk," that is, into society?[6] What would it look like if large numbers of people argued that appeals to rationality masked the exercise of power? What moments might open up for the reconsideration of what genuine rationality might entail? What would happen if significant numbers of educated people thought that rationality itself ought to be abandoned?

Might one not expect societies in which groups of people talk past one another? Might one not expect surges in popularity, and then sudden turning away from, not only specific people but institutions and principles? Might one not expect to see different bids to occupy the calmest, most unassuming spaces, only to find those places erupt in contest? Might one not expect to find tremendous outpourings of enthusiasm and hope, then in the next moment reports of terrible deception and anger?

To characterize one's own time is fraught with risks. Yet it is necessary to do so. If one's vision of the humanities and social sciences, and especially the people who pass through them, does not sweep one's own time up into

---

6. See the book's epigraph on p. viii.

itself, then truly what does it offer? Many people are confused about the status of rationality in contemporary society and do not have a sense of the options before them regarding what rationality might mean. On the one hand, it may seem that the question is esoteric at a time when many issues confronting society are tangible and immediate; on the other, though, the question of rationality's status may be one of the most important that the university as an institution asks. Theory is one of the spaces in that institution where this happens, or at least can.

Rationality, Theory, and Language

The conversation organizes itself around language. In the nineteenth century, the paradigm for what was knowable and worthy of study came from the sciences. For more than two hundred years science had been in the ascendant, its methods and assumptions dominating what rationality itself looked like. For its part, English as a discipline privileged interest in the language itself as part of a scientific way of proceeding. English departments took shape in the collecting of *specimens* of English literature. The aim was twofold: to collect examples of literature written at different times; and to advance the scientific study of philology, including how the language itself had evolved. The study of language was indeed important, but not nearly as central as it would come to be.

Developments in philosophical thinking in the twentieth century helped to change the situation. One important school of thought announced the importance of the everyday. It came to be realized, by continental European thinkers especially, that our experience of the world has an existential dimension. Language plays an integral role. Our being *in* the world impinges itself on all our would-be claims *about* the world. No one gets the view from nowhere. This recognition (in fact a *rediscovery* of a very old view) had profound implications for science, at least for any pretense the latter may have had to being a master discourse or final arbiter regarding the nature of rationality.

Such developments were and remain good news for lovers of literature, which has always recognized the complexity of what it might mean to say that humans are rational creatures. Stories, poems, and dramas immerse their audiences and readers in a narrative or life-world; they are highly convertible with the philosophical appreciation of everyday life, human situatedness, and language. Greek epics, for example, begin *in medias res* (in the middle of things). The Greeks appreciated the limitations placed on our perspectives, as well as on our powers; they referred to the failure to recognize such limits as *hubris* or pride. Mainstream literary theory builds on this ancient literary awareness of our being in the middle of things, though it also transforms it.

Some introductions to literary theory start with a description of one or two of the ways people were encouraged to read in the early twentieth century. At that time, literature had begun to supplant philology, while modern theory had not yet developed. Such textbooks approach their subject this way to establish a contrast, to set the jewel of theory against the foil of only slightly older reading practices and assumptions. They then introduce the famous work in linguistics that underpins theory's massive philosophical concerns with language, before proceeding to introduce all the different theories about literature indebted to this development.

This book takes a different approach. It holds back the question of language and its role in the development of literary theory. It does so not to make the question of language optional or incidental—it isn't. Rather, it takes the view that to encounter theory in terms of rationality prepares one to track the technical legacy of language theorists more effectively. It begins, accordingly, with the redescription of rationality in several contemporary theories.

In other words, we can start where we are. Feminism, critical race theory, and Freudian psychoanalysis are either so current or so embedded in our cultural consciousness as to be familiar and accessible to all readers from the outset. One can readily see in them a concern with the nature of rationality. They attack what the philosophical tradition in the West had pretty much taken for granted since the time of Plato and Aristotle. What appears to be rational and self-evident, say from a masculine perspective or from a white Anglo-American one, is not necessarily so from any number of other points of view. Once familiar with the evident concern with rationality as a problematic category, the reader will then better appreciate how the interrogation of language took shape and intensifies the critique.

Because the attack on rationality itself is so comprehensive in feminism, critical race theory, and Freudian psychoanalysis, the second section of the argument—before tracking the development of mainstream theory—will examine a different approach. This section introduces a set of reference points as well as a discussion that insists on the rightness of the critique, especially of the pretenses of science. At the same time, it preserves rationality as a meaningful category when taken in an enlarged sense. In doing so, it challenges not only commonplace assumptions about the status of scientific rationality, but also how art, literature, and the study of history must conduct themselves as alternatives to it.

The third and final section of this book then traces the concern with rationality to some of its roots in language. Three such critiques include the thought of the nineteenth-century figure Friedrich Nietzsche; the previously mentioned early twentieth-century work in linguistics; and the theoretical movement that began to take hold in the 1960s.

Not the Last Word

The focus in this book is on introducing one central theme in literary theory rather than many theories or much terminology. It is on helping readers to see, through a select number of those theories, their orientation towards a critique of rationality. Development of terminology and of specialized, technical argumentation can be deferred. Once readers see for themselves the focus on the problem of rationality in contemporary theories, they can then fold in more technical and abstruse considerations.

Literary theory is a sub-discipline of literary studies. It helps to accentuate the literary critique of rationality and to show how that literary concern intersects with that of other disciplines. Various conceptions of what counts as rational, especially in the modern era, exhibit profound limitations. One can nonetheless deepen one's commitment to rationality as a key dimension of what it means to be human.

To say that rationality is the essence of literary theory is not to attempt to dispel mystery. It is not to claim the last word, either about theory or about the nature of rationality. It is in fact to invite one further into the mysterious depths of our experience of reality. Someone has written that

> if a man, therefore, in his philosophical inquiry, gropes after the essence of things, he finds himself, by the very act of approaching his object, in an unfathomable abyss, but it is an abyss of *light*.[7]

Our experience of reality is such that the earnest and disciplined application of rationality is itself bound up with mystery: we recognize an abyss, though it is an abyss of light. Rationality does not empty out in conquest and manipulation; rather, it over and over again reinforces the sense of a mystery at

---

7. Pieper, *The Silence of St. Thomas*, 96.

the heart of things. As we will see, for some commentators the pursuit of the essence of anything binds rationality together with love.

Too many people in the humanities have invoked theory to conclude that humans make their own meaning rather than participate in its making. In this view, the world itself is not meaningful and there is no ultimate source of meaning because the universe is a chance product of material events. There is no tower of Truth, to borrow Langland's image.[8] There is no meaning beyond brute matter. Some celebrate the "acid" of naturalism.[9] Rationality gives way to willing alone. A world without meaning, though, is a world without hope. Where literature is concerned, beauty is at best a pleasing illusion, at worst a deception. The capacity of art to contribute to our understanding of universal truth, meanwhile, is non-existent and irrelevant. Language, for its part, can be nothing more than a tool. It may be useful for building a better world or for the purposes of manipulation, but ultimately is nothing more than a tool either way . . . because there is no meaning in the world of which it might itself be an expression.

It's hard to say how widespread such a view is. Common goodwill recoils from the cynicism implicit in the notion that we entirely make meaning. However, even if one rejects skepticism, how much has been gained if one subordinates the search for meaning and the yearning for self-transcendence to the demands of day-to-day life? These are endless, not least for the student. At some point, metaphysical considerations impinge themselves.

This book invites readers to see theory as an undertaking that can help to rescue and to broaden what rationality can and ought to mean. As such, it can contribute powerfully to our understanding of literature and art. The latter are bound up with who we are as rational creatures. At the same time, they are deeply consonant with the appreciation of mystery and with yearnings beyond ourselves.

The poet Seamus Heaney offers the following affirmation of truth in a reflection on poetry:

> . . . literariness as such is not an abdication from the truth. The literary is one of the methods human beings have devised for getting at reality. . . . Its diversions are not to be taken as deceptions but as roads less travelled by where the country we thought we knew

---

8. Again, from the epigraph.
9. Dennett, *Darwin's Dangerous Idea*, 63.

is seen again in a new and revealing light. A simpler light, maybe, but still a true one.[10]

Heaney does not shy away from using the words "true," "reality," and "light" as if they referred to something that could be held in common, nor does he shy away from pressing the relevance of literature in such a context. His statement may be puzzling and awkward to some. It can serve as a beacon in the study of the subject matter of this book, or perhaps as a stubborn rock in the pathway. As a beacon, it provides reassurance and hope; as a rock, it may unsettle those who would reduce art to subjectivism, a "theorized" relativism, or a philosophical skepticism.

A second, closing, quotation from a philosopher of language likewise encourages one to appreciate the place of literature and art within society:

> No artist of the religiously vital cultures of the past ever produced his work of art with any other intention than that his creation should be received in terms of what it says and presents and that it should have its place in the world where men live together.[11]

The artist has always intended to speak and to be heard for what he or she has to say where people gather together. Ideas about art have an important role to play; they influence a society's self-understanding and its direction. The arts are not simply for private amusement; they have the capacity to speak to us collectively. They enlarge our ongoing dialogue about and enactment of what it means to be human. While they challenge harmful assumptions about what counts as rationality, they do not subvert rationality altogether.

The discussion of literary theory in the pages that follow invites the reader to approach this sub-discipline with this central tension in mind: whether rationality is really something else in disguise, or our commitment to it is to be chastened and deepened through reflection on literature and the arts.

---

10. Heaney, "Eclogues," 4.
11. Gadamer, "Universality," 4–5.

The Critique of Rationality
in Literature and Theory

1

The Critique of Rationality in Literature

Introduction

Literary theory offers an intensive critique of the notion of rationality. The writings of theorists can be challenging to follow and their technical terminology difficult to learn. Nonetheless, the ordinary reader of literature can readily identify a commonality between their central concern and a prominent theme in literary works of all kinds. Stories, poetry, and drama regularly interrogate what we think we know, how we know, and what it means to think of ourselves as rational beings.

This chapter offers four examples from the world of poetry to show the reader of literature that they're really on home turf when they turn from thinking about poems to thinking about theory. The first comes from the opening paragraphs of a book on the art of writing poetry. Three poems follow, one on law, one on solving an agricultural problem, one that begins with the phrase "How do they do it . . . ?" From a number of directions, all four of these pieces challenge the reader to reconsider what they think rationality entails. In other words, the student of English and the lover of literature ought to feel that they can access the principal theme of this book. In important ways, it is "home grown"; the central concern of literary theory is evident in the study of literature itself.

Advice about Poetry

Jack Myers, a distinguished American poet, taught the craft of writing poetry and in 2004 published *The Portable Poetry Workshop*. The first sentence of this book challenges any straightforward understanding of "rationality": "The very aim of art—to fix the ineffable—is a paradoxical, impossible, and yet sacred task."[1] To call the aim of art "a paradoxical, impossible, and yet sacred task" at one and the same time pushes past the limits of reason and declares meaningfulness. The short phrase "fix the ineffable" names the paradox by combining the notion of stability with spirituality. To "fix" in this context implies pinning down, like skewering a butterfly specimen to put it under glass. The latter activity has some level of importance for the taxonomist or beginner botanist. Yet one instinctively recognizes a limitation, if not a contradiction, in the practice of taking a living creature and pinning it to a piece of cardboard.

The ineffable: well, what is that? An offset quotation from Mark Strand, another poet, gives Myers (and us) a little help. Strand deploys the following phrase to describe what poetry tries to articulate: "'something that lies at the heart of experience but cannot be pointed out or described without being altered or diminished.'"[2] That's a pretty good definition of the ineffable, one that acknowledges the reality of something yet at the same time distances it from the world of signs and intellectual activity. This aspect of reality "'cannot be *pointed out* or *described*,'" at least not without its being "'altered or diminished.'"

Somehow art goes in both directions at once. It helps to fix things, to make them identifiable and accessible; it also preserves their strangeness. Poetry is language, so there's some effort at communication, at manifesting the inner. Yet it mocks "'one's desire for reduction, for plain and available order.'"[3] Note the distancing from science in the references to "'reduction'" and to "'plain and available order.'" Strand is blunt: "'It is not *knowledge* that poetry contains . . . .'"[4] That's a bold statement; one does well to sit with it for a moment.

Strand immediately pulls back from a complete disavowal of a link between poetry and knowledge: "'. . . at least not as I conceive knowledge,'" he adds.[5] He seems to suggest that the problem may rest with *his own* way of conceiving things. He leaves room for positive words that have something to do with our getting traction on the so-called real world by referring to an "'occasion for belief,'" "'reason for assent,'" an "'avowal of being.'" These are all very positive phrases, and they all sound like reasonable outcomes from

---

1. Myers, *Portable Poetry Workshop*, vii.
2. Myers, *Portable Poetry Workshop*, vii.
3. Myers, *Portable Poetry Workshop*, vii.
4. Myers, *Portable Poetry Workshop*, vii, emphasis mine.
5. Myers, *Portable Poetry Workshop*, vii.

having spent time acquiring knowledge. They sound like reasonable outcomes from having spent a term studying poetry, for example. At the same time, Strand warns us off a sense of *revelation*: "'It is not knowledge because it is never revealed.'"[6] Revelation in this context is synonymous with certain knowledge, but, on the other hand, he encourages affirmation.

In the next paragraph, Myers refers to Strand again to push back some more against exaggerated skepticism about poetry and the arts. Through poetry, we get the sense of something being satisfied. We also get the recognition that, without art, we are left with "'silence or banality,'"[7] some lack, some failure of concordance with the way things really are. Silence doesn't really satisfy, because we want to be able to *share* our experiences. Banality refers to humdrum speech, the sort of thing one might say about the quality of coffee at McDonald's or about what one did yesterday evening. Lots of our experiences, however, rise above the banal, and we want to be able to talk about them with some precision, liveliness, and meaning. Even drinking coffee at McDonald's can qualify.

Taking the reins back from Strand, Myers briefly becomes effusive about practicalities and specificities, forms of knowing and rational control, related to poetry. The art form is described in terms of "a highly technical legacy"; it exhibits a terminology that "rivals those found in the domain of a *science*."[8] In other words, there *is* a place for technical knowing, as well as for highly calibrated engagement of subject matter on the part of the poet. Myers is keen to affirm that level of intellectual activity. Yet the author soon returns to the wisdom of another poet, one reminding us (again) that a poem is not a "manipulable . . . pattern" but an "unduplicatable resonance."[9]

The back and forth movement in these opening paragraphs has *something* to do with knowledge and rationality, but clearly an unexamined definition of reason, or practicality, or relevance to ordinary experience, will not do. Significantly, words like "'belief,'" "sacred,' and "'revealed'" have come over the horizon. They also occupy places in the spectrum running from skepticism about rationality to its affirmation. The person who undertakes to acquire some skill in writing poetry and, in turn, in reading it, learns very quickly that they have entered into an activity requiring skill,

---

6. Myers, *Portable Poetry Workshop*, vii.
7. Myers, *Portable Poetry Workshop*, vii.
8. Myers, *Portable Poetry Workshop*, vii, emphasis mine.
9. Myers, *Portable Poetry Workshop*, viii.

knowledge, and intellectual training, among other things. Yet rationality itself has become something of a puzzle.

The Critique of Rationality in Three Poems

What Law Reveals

None of this will overly surprise the student of art or of poetry, especially once they have been at it for a while. One can see these issues in specific poems. The following examples take up aspects of rationality to put it under pressure. We find ourselves wondering whether characters in the poems really have taken the right approach to the problem at hand. Yet the situations don't easily resolve themselves. They cannot be sorted out with banal explanations. Puzzles remain that fire our intellectual imagination in various ways. Seamus Heaney's "The Outlaw," Maxine Kumin's "Woodchucks," and Sharon Olds's "Sex without Love" probe limits of understanding and expose a logic that runs in strange directions.

"The Outlaw" appeals to the sphere of law. By implication, it posits a lawfulness that makes sense, establishes a stable and rational point of reference. Yet that notion becomes problematic in the course of the poem. Several figures seem to occupy positions somehow outside the law, though in different ways. The point of reference keeps shifting:

> Kelly's kept an unlicensed bull, well away
> From the road: you risked fine but had to pay
>
> The normal fee if cows were serviced there. (1–3)

The unlicensed bull in some sense qualifies as an "outlaw" and is explicitly referred to as such in the second to last line of the poem (23). He is used to inseminate or to service cows. Yet in what meaningful sense can the bull be called an outlaw? Isn't he just an animal? Isn't the sex act just natural for him? Heaney brings into focus the question of what law, what rationality, *means* relative to nature.

Surely the real outlaw here is Kelly, who makes his bull available for insemination without adhering to bureaucratic regulations. Or what about the speaker, who has brought a cow for servicing? "Once I dragged a nervous Friesian on a tether . . ." (4). It doesn't take long for Heaney to pique our interest in the speaker, who seems to be projecting his own nervousness. His anxiety doesn't appear to be limited to the issue of the legality of the transaction: "I gave Old Kelly the clammy silver" (7) sounds straightforward enough, but soon he is watching "the business-like conception" (10) from his "lofty station" (9). The language, suggestive of transactional detachment and objectification, descends into the mechanistic and the violent in the description of the bull's actions:

> The illegal sire fumbled from his stall
>
> Unhurried as an old steam engine shunting,
> He circled, snored and nosed. No hectic panting,
>
> Just the unfussy ease of a good tradesman,
> Then an awkward, unexpected jump, and
>
> His knobbed forelegs straddling her flank,
> He slammed life home, impassive as a tank . . . (12–18)

The speaker has expectations ("no hectic panting"); he is watching and learning. His choice of images, however, suggests a disposition in which rationality is at odds with ideals of what sex can be, at least in the human sphere. If he is learning, he's learning very particular lessons, and it's not clear why he's fixating on this and not that. Mechanics and violence dominate his perspective: sex is "just" these things. In the end, he too has received some sort of troubling satisfaction. He has observed, he has learned, what sex *really* consists of, apparently. Strangely, it has given him release. Having led the cow to be serviced on a taut rope, he's not in a hurry now: "I walked ahead of her, the rope now slack" (22).

Whatever the speaker has discovered, the reader holds him and his perspective at arm's length. The episode suggests a dark hinterland to the world of rationality. Heaney accompanies the speaker in this shadowy terrain formally too. The presentation in tidily separated rhyming couplets encourages the sense of a baseline clarity. The couplet form is itself traditional and predictable. By twentieth-century standards it is naïve and juvenile, like a rationality that can explain everything neatly. Whatever expectations of order the poem promises visually, they break down quickly. Enjambment eats away at the superficially separated couplets, pushing the poem in the direction of narrative and of complicated life.

The question is, is life *irrational* and is Heaney claiming that it is so? Does an apparent desire to understand cause violence to proliferate in our representations of reality, as with the speaker here—"whacked" (11), "slammed," "a tank," "a tipped-up load of sand" (19)? Is the situation portentous? Will the speaker later enact imitations of this re-presentation of what he perceives sex to be, this language used to describe it? The effort at description reveals dimensions within the speaker that he does not seem to recognize, a limitation in self-knowledge that offers no reassurance regarding how he might act. Through him, Heaney opens up the question of such a limitation within all of us and its possible ramifications. Are we the outlaw too?

Obsession and Rationalization

"Woodchucks," a poem by the American Jewish poet Maxine Kumin, starts out sensibly enough, if one can get past the odd first word "Gassing." It seems to be addressing the problem of how to get rid of garden pests:

> Gassing the woodchucks didn't turn out right.
> The knockout bomb from the Feed and Grain Exchange
> was featured as merciful, quick at the bone
> and the case we had against them was airtight,
> both exits shoehorned shut with puddingstone,
> but they had a sub-sub-basement out of range. (1–6)

It just about makes sense that one might have to do this to animals. At least the solution was "merciful." Yet the tone doesn't sit right, too jaunty, too casual under any circumstances, with phrases like "knockout bomb," the pun on "airtight," and the smug alliterative satisfaction of "exits shoehorned shut." The reasonable has wandered uncomfortably near to the sadistic.

"The case we had against them" (another law metaphor) sounds increasingly like rationalization. The five-stanza poem reads like a five-act play, with the normality escalating to the point where, in the pivotal third stanza, the situation unleashes in the speaker an irrational, self-justifying zeal:

> righteously thrilling
> to the feel of the .22, the bullets' neat noses. (13–14)

The excess has heightened the speaker's acuity. Visually, the poem slips into the mathematical precision of a number (replete with decimal point), followed by a return to language that strives to equal cold numeracy with the bluntness of the /b/, and the triple alliteration of repeated /t/, /n/, and razing /z/. In this context, righteousness reads like a synonym for an untroubled rationality that doesn't take into account the complexity of human relationships with the rest of creation, let alone the darkness of the human urge for purity and unhinged compulsion. The speaker sees "the littlest woodchuck's face" (17), takes in "the everbearing roses" (18), relishes the mother woodchuck flipflopping in the air. Hyper-rationality, as indicated by the precise, detached observations, the numbers, and the self-justifications, has become irrational.

This version of making sense of the world offers no escape or resolution: there is forever "one chuck left" (25). The desire for racial purity that gripped Nazi Germany, a supposedly highly developed and enlightened European power, exposes a compulsion that can't be reasoned with. The movement from "Gassing" in the first line to "gassed underground the quiet Nazi way" (30) in the last reminds the reader of what has been done by some humans to others and cannot be undone. This horrific chapter in Western European history seeps into all philosophical reflection on the meaning of "enlightenment," "humanism," and "progress" in the second half of the twentieth century. It has induced some thinkers to turn their backs on rationality altogether.

Lovers as Factors

Sharon Olds's "Sex without Love" begins, in its title, with a straightforward description, as if of an ordinary reality and possibility: sex as an act separable from love as an emotion. In connection with this flat statement, the first half of the poem nonetheless expresses astonishment and doubt (of the order I-wish-I-could-do-that). The second half settles into an ironclad conviction predicated on the isolated individual and the goal of self-protection. From a certain perspective, this outlook makes sense.

The poem opens with a question:

> How do they do it, the ones who make love
> without love? (1–2)

The first half of the opening line on its own suggests ambiguously a tone of marvel or awe and also the sensibility of the earnest would-be practitioner. Rationality in this context takes the form of know-how, practical reason, getting the knack for something. The rest of the line makes this earnest inquiry momentarily ridiculous: "How do they do it, the ones who make love . . . ?" There *are* countless magazines and therapy books, but asking for guidance on how to make love, full stop (or at least end-of-line)? Isn't it natural? Don't ya kinda just gotta get in there and do it? The speaker comes across as more than a little naïve and bookish. Perhaps she is asking the question as an innocent child.

Enjambment makes the first phrase of the second line land in the poem like an astonishing qualifier. One cannot yet tell whether the speaker is repulsed or impressed by an ability she has apparently observed. However, she no longer strikes the reader as really young or merely naïve. The next word, "Beautiful" (2), suggests that she is impressed, but by the end of the sentence, the reader is left wondering if they have just witnessed passion or brutal, cold-as-ice dismemberment. All in all, the inquiry reads like an outsider expressing a desire that gives them intense voyeuristic pleasure:

> How do they come to the
>
> come to the come to the God come to the (8–9)

A poem that begins with an earnest question and proceeds with exquisite syntax momentarily abandons conventional sentence structure, only to return to redoubled order and control, linguistic and otherwise.

By the second half of the poem, the possibility of sex without love has emerged as the genuine ideal and the poem settles into a syntactically clear and precise statement. Given nihilistic premises of aloneness and meaninglessness, it valorizes the only sensible conclusions. Those who can truly hold on to them are impressive:

> These are the true religious,
>
> the purists, the pros, the ones who will not
>
> accept a false Messiah, love the
>
> priest instead of the God. (13–16)

They do not make the mistake of misdirected worship. No one pulls the wool over their eyes. They look out for their own interests, knowing they are alone in the universe:

> They do not
>
> mistake the lover for their own pleasure,
>
> they are like great runners: they know they are alone (16–18)

Olds offers another great line-ending here (in the longest line of the poem): "alone" leads out into the nothingness of the white space of the page. In this environment, one truly has only what one controls: the inanimate, or what one can reduce to "factors" (21). These are one's only companions, "the road surface, the cold, the wind, / the fit of their shoes, their overall cardio- / vascular health—just factors . . ." (19–21). One must strive to reduce others to this status as well. That is the goal of lovemaking.

Yet this compelling logic comes under pressure in the way the opening tone of marvel lingers. The speaker seems to be trying to talk herself into the rectitude of an attitude she can clearly articulate. Personal doubts remain. There's irony, too, in the assertion that the self-lovers are "the true religious." Their certainty, in the world of the poem, comes off as belief. The speaker's doubt, meanwhile, registers as hope, not only that it might be okay to give ourselves in vulnerability and love to another, but also that we mightn't be alone in the cosmos, leading isolated and meaningless lives. Hope challenges a certain kind of ironclad "rationality" that only tendentiously gets to parade itself as courageous, unflinching, honest. Residually, the poem hints that such hope may, after all, be as rational. In a world of cold and objective rationality, moral categories are supposedly sealed in a separate category; in reality, though, moral thinking weaves its way into human argumentation and experience.

Conclusion

Poetry puts pressure on rationality, on what we think we know for sure, *how* we think we know, and the various systems that we have in place for getting through life with a semblance of control and dignity. Yet in the examples considered, it's not clear that the writers would take rationality or meaningfulness itself away from us. It's not clear they aren't attacking as partial what we variously set in place as the true and comprehensive guide we can rely on. Rationality itself might not be the problem, only what we conceive it to be or how much we invest in it.

Rationality, at this point, remains frustratingly difficult to define or pin down. In mainstream literary theory, the meaning of the term depends in large part on the theoretical perspective being considered. In the rest of the chapters in this section, we will consider three pejorative definitions of rationality from the perspective of three different theories. For feminists, rationality is male; for race theorists, rationality is white;

for psychoanalysts, rationality is repression. For some groups, men perhaps, or white people, it may seem that what *they* think is obvious, logical, and foundational is likewise taken for granted by everyone, or should be. Feminists, race theorists, and psychoanalysts, however, have shown that what variously masquerades as rational is only, at best, partial. At worst, it masks a bid for manipulation and power, even if the practitioner remains unaware of their own complicity. Very often, that is the case.

After these three powerful contemporary forms of theory have been considered, we will take stock. By that point, the reader will be able to identify and to appreciate this guiding concern of theorists in general. The reader wanting a basic introduction to theory will already be in a position to recognize what animates it.

2

Rationality Is Male

Introduction

There's so much at stake in raising the issue of "rationality" that doing so can seem, from the casual onlooker's point of view, overwhelming, ill-advised, and perhaps unjustified. Precisely here, one may encounter their first point of confusion, because they don't quite believe that the situation is being described properly. Common sense seems to speak against the notion that reason itself could be challenged. Yet literary theory in some ways merely intensifies a line of questioning that runs through literature itself. Perhaps the dislodging of a stable point of reference will reveal a misplaced or hardened confidence and open up new possibilities, or the recovery of old ones.

So here we are, beginning an introductory analysis of theory almost at random with one of its many popular forms, feminism (or, as we shall see in a moment, feminisms). The leading anthology of literary theory being brought into dialogue throughout this book says the following in its introduction to this theory: "only by questioning the status of the subject of Feminism—'woman'—does a feminist criticism avoid replicating the masculinist cultural error of taking the dominant for the universal."[1] A few paragraphs on, with reference to one specific theorist, the editors write that "matter ... is irreducible to male Western conceptuality" and that matter is "impossible to assimilate to male reason."[2] A couple of paragraphs on from there, now with a different form of feminism in mind, they write that "What lies outside male reason is precisely everything such reason abhors—contradiction, nonidentity, fluidity, non-rationality, illogicality,

---

1. Rivkin and Ryan, *Literary Theory*, 765/893.
2. Rivkin and Ryan, *Literary Theory*, 767/895.

mixing of genres, etc."[3] And a few lines below that, they refer to "the hierarchical orders of male rationalist philosophy."[4] All of these phrases are working interchangeably. Note the terms "conceptuality" and "reason" especially as synonyms of rationality. Note also the reference to the idea of the "universal" in this context.

The task here is not, at the moment, to nail down whether the editors believe that there *is* such a thing as rationality as a meaningful category. When they refer to "*such* reason" (my emphasis) it seems as though "male reason" may be only a *perversion* of the real thing. Yet when they then describe what lies outside "such reason" as "*non*-rationality" (my emphasis), it seems that "such reason" may be co-terminous with *all* reason. Similarly, when they describe "taking the dominant for the universal" as "the masculinist cultural error," they *may* be leaving room for "the universal." It's just that "male reason" can't access it. The term "universal" here is a near-equivalent to "rationality."

The point, for these purveyors of feminist thought, is that when many people appeal to "rationality," what they're actually referring to is something that has been established by men and serves male interests. Within the context of a discussion generated by feminist concerns, it is not an exaggeration to say "rationality is male." To say so is to commit oneself to something other, some other way of being, some reality (e.g., matter), some way of thinking, that doesn't assume that thinking itself is unproblematic. Thinking, given historical developments, is very problematic. It isn't neutral. From a feminist perspective, it looks very male.

Feminism

In their introduction, Julie Rivkin and Michael Ryan *start* by emphasizing the plurality of feminisms. This move is itself noteworthy. It announces a theme to be traced as *Rationality Is* . . . progresses: a plurality of perspectives, positions, identities. The other move they make at the outset is to sketch a history. Feminism develops and changes over time as it encounters various other ideas. Please note that they take as their starting point "the late 1960s and early 1970s."[5] I wish to begin a timeline and to focus for now

---

3. Rivkin and Ryan, *Literary Theory*, 767/895.
4. Rivkin and Ryan, *Literary Theory*, 767/895.
5. Rivkin and Ryan, *Literary Theory*, 765/893.

on part of the twentieth century. Over and over the importance of the late 1960s and early 1970s will be apparent.

> the mid-twentieth century → the late 1960s and the early 1970s → the subsequent development of literary theory from the late 1960s onward

For now, as a starting point, in an effort to understand the necessity and nature of theory from a feminist point of view, a twofold reality identified by Adrienne Rich can be emphasized: "the history of women's oppression and the silencing of their voices."[6] As Rivkin and Ryan point out, in literary studies, early feminism took as its task confronting oppressive stereotypes in literature being written by men, and overcoming silence by recovering works written by women: "This early period is sometimes described as having two stages, one concerned with the critique of misogynist stereotypes in male literature, the other devoted to the recovery of a lost tradition and to the long labor of historical reconstruction."[7]

For many years, English literature was assumed to have a stable *canon* or set of "must-read" books. These were almost entirely written by men, promoted a male perspective, and perpetuated male ideas about what counted as "great literature," "aesthetics," "beauty," and "style." The word "canon" became synonymous with "rationality" as *an appeal to an objective standard*. For feminists, the canon was anything but disinterested. Male approaches and male selections needed to be countered by an explicit gynocriticism, literary criticism done by women and on female authors. It should be noted, though, that all along feminists have recognized that some male writers actively work against stereotypes or stable conceptions of women in their works. Geoffrey Chaucer and James Joyce have been considered exemplary figures in this regard.

Rivkin and Ryan identify two main strands of feminism since those early days. Essentialists make arguments based on physical differences between men and women. Luce Irigaray makes the powerful and rather poetic argument that women are more directly linked to material nature. (An excerpt from Irigaray's writings is discussed below.) To be male is to be in flight from such contact with matter in the direction of abstraction, to be in the habit of treating nature as an object and seeking to dominate it. For Irigaray, there is an essential difference between being male and being

6. Rivkin and Ryan, *Literary Theory*, 765/894.
7. Rivkin and Ryan, *Literary Theory*, 766/894.

female. This characterization at the very least provides a way of imagining the limitations of rationality, of recognizing potential blindspots when the power of reason is accepted uncritically. Furthermore, essentialist arguments like Irigaray's *play an important role historically*. Other insights have come into view in part because of the ground gained by essentialism in linking the female with the material, with something other than rationality, abstraction, and objectification.

Rivkin and Ryan draw attention to a problem with identifying women with matter, one that led to a further development in feminism: a split between essentialists and constructivists. While essentialists are happy to accept an identification of women with materiality, constructivists are not. The latter are prompted to speculate that *gender identity itself* is a product of patriarchal culture: "The psychology or identity that feminist essentialists think is different from men's is merely the product of conditioning under patriarchy."[8] Constructivists argue just as persuasively that the very idea of "nature," like that of gender or even "matter," develops in a cultural context and "is fabricated."[9]

The passive voice of the grammatical construction "is fabricated" is relevant here. Who or what is doing the fabricating remains deliberately unclear in constructivism. Part of the emphasis in constructivism lies in recognizing the pervasiveness of forces that are constantly at work and cannot be isolated and quarantined, even for purposes of identification. This difficulty points in the direction of language. As Rivkin and Ryan say in summary of constructivism, "Feminist literary criticism moves with time from the criticism of writing by men and the exploration of writing by women to a questioning of what it means at all to engage with or in language."[10] Language is always doing work to shape our perceptions. The emerging emphasis on language in this discussion of feminism can serve us as a reminder of the importance of the final section of this book.

The difference between the two schools of thought—essentialism and constructivism—is so pronounced in Rivkin and Ryan's opinion that "there was no possible meeting of minds between the two, for each necessarily denied the other."[11] Their position represents the mainstream

---

8. Rivkin and Ryan, *Literary Theory*, 768/896.
9. Rivkin and Ryan, *Literary Theory*, 768/896.
10. Rivkin and Ryan, *Literary Theory*, 769/897.
11. Rivkin and Ryan, *Literary Theory*, 767/895.

view.[12] The claim that there is no possible meeting of minds, however, is not unassailable. For instance, historically speaking, essentialism partly enables the development of constructivism, as has already been noted. The force of Rivkin and Ryan's own historical argument is weakened when they downplay the importance of the former. The issue of the general relationship between essentialism and constructivism will be considered in more detail later in the book.

At any rate, one does well to appreciate the force of Irigaray's logic, and her sensitivity to *where* the problem lies. For the novice tempted by the either/or language of Rivkin and Ryan and perhaps intimidated by constructivism, she is easily misunderstood. Nevertheless, Irigaray draws attention to the uses of rationality in a compelling way.

Feminism is one of the foundational and most important forms of literary theory. Renowned theorist Terry Eagleton has written, "Feminism has not only transformed the cultural landscape but . . . has become the very model of morality for our time."[13] In a very concrete, political, and practical way, feminism focalizes the question, what are we assuming when we appeal to logic, to reason, to a universal standard? Often we can easily see that what at first appeared to be objective serves male interests.

From here, one can go on to ask similar questions in terms of other considerations, such as race or disability or respect for animals. Feminism can help a person to pause and reflect on what is being assumed when one assumes or insists on their own neutrality. Whatever one's commitments in terms of gender or race, political affiliation, class, or even academic discipline, this lesson applies.

Mimicry and Masculine Logic

Luce Irigaray outlines a powerful feminist goal and feminist strategy in "The Power of Discourse and the Subordination of the Feminine." These are of enduring relevance, both for a historical understanding of feminism and for a deep appreciation of current trends and issues. The goal for Irigaray is to "explode" male conceptuality, male discourse. The strategy is to make a

---

12. Rivkin and Ryan have dropped this reading by Irigaray from the third edition of their anthology. She may have become too embarrassing as their own commitments as constructivists have become more deeply entrenched.

13. Eagleton, *After Theory*, 7.

performance out of mimicking male expectations and ideas of the female. How she arrives at this strategy is extremely interesting!

Irigaray associates the Western philosophical tradition with male abstraction. The opposite of this practice is the female association with matter. It would seem that these two are like chalk and cheese, so how is the female to find a voice and to thrive in a male world? Irigaray's advice takes into account the falsity of assuming that reason is neutral. She writes,

> One must assume the feminine role deliberately. Which means already to convert a form of subordination into an affirmation, and thus to begin to thwart it. Whereas a direct feminine challenge to this condition means demanding to speak as a (masculine) "subject," that is, it means to postulate a relation to the intelligible that would maintain sexual difference.[14]

"One must assume the feminine role deliberately...," she writes. This statement can lead one to make two separate and seemingly obvious points. Given that theory urges an alternative to the status quo, not to mention the fact that the topic is feminism specifically, one might assume that by "the feminine role" Irigaray means some preunderstood *alternative* to male expectations and projections of what a woman should be. Secondly, the word "deliberately" seems to reinforce the sense of a stubborn and forceful commitment to that alternative, whatever it may be.

Irigaray is saying something different. To "assume the feminine role" is to play the role expected of one as a woman, that is, the role expected by male conceptuality. When she goes on to say, "Which means already to convert a form of subordination into an affirmation...," she is claiming that subversive work is *already underway*, despite appearances to the contrary. Specifically, subordination becomes its opposite. How can this be?

She is advocating what she calls mimicry, deliberate imitation. The crucial point is *why* she advocates this strategy. Her argument here is little short of brilliant; it opens up a vista of enduring relevance for all theoretical thinking. She argues that if one tries to oppose the male position with a counter-*argument*, one has already committed oneself to working within the male philosophical tradition: "Whereas a direct feminine challenge to this condition means demanding to speak as a (masculine) subject." "A direct feminine challenge" involves accepting male categories. It is to work from within male conceptuality. As I say, I think this insight is little short of brilliant.

14. Irigaray, "Power of Discourse," 795.

To mimic, however, is *to make visible what cannot otherwise be seen.* The strategy is a little like the effective everyday approach in friendly (or not-so-friendly) debate of repeating back to someone what they have said so that they can hear themselves. Often that's enough to get them to qualify their position. The act of mimicry also makes clear that the one performing the action *is elsewhere.* Their identity is not exhausted by the function that they take on. Furthermore, it involves postulating "a relation to the intelligible that would maintain sexual difference." The realm of the intelligible is the realm of rationality. The relation to it is, through mimicry, a relation of difference, maintaining difference relative to the intelligible.

This practice leads Irigaray to make a further bold claim: that in occupying the elsewhere of matter, women actually make speculation (that is, rational activity) possible. Irigaray says that the latter is actually and ironically dependent on the former. Mimicry (or mimesis) has the capacity to help male speculation to realize that it (the speculation) has been generated by matter in the first place: "Mother-matter-nature must go on forever nourishing speculation."[15] The paragraphs that follow in her essay repeat the logic of mimicry. They lead to the threefold claim that mimicry "[jams] the theoretical machinery,"[16] produces a "*disruptive excess,*"[17] and "explodes every firmly established form, figure, idea or concept."[18]

Irigaray helps any would-be theorist to get at the problem of working within a framework that one unwittingly accepts without question. To fight fire with fire by opposing male ideas and arguments with counterarguments amounts to a failure to recognize the ground on which one stands. Such a tactic amounts to a lack of self-knowledge, as well as a failure to reckon with the difficulty of achieving change. Mimicry can look, to the uninitiated, like capitulation and weakness. Yet it has built into it the stubbornness of appealing to an elsewhere that male conceptuality cannot imagine, certainly not without feminists' help.

---

15. Irigaray, "Power of Discourse," 796.
16. Irigaray, "Power of Discourse," 796.
17. Irigaray, "Power of Discourse," 796, emphasis hers.
18. Irigaray, "Power of Discourse," 797.

The Stupid Suburban Housewife in "Bluebeard's Egg"

Margaret Atwood is a contemporary Canadian writer of short stories, novels, poetry, and essays. She is now perhaps best known for her adapted novel *The Handmaid's Tale*, but her place in Canadian letters has been growing since the early 1970s. Atwood's short story "Bluebeard's Egg" appears in a 1983 collection of the same name. The story mimics prevailing stereotypes of the time to offer a sympathetic, hopeful sketch of a bored, upper-middle-class suburban housewife. As the story closes, we see her lying in bed, suppressing the almost certain awareness that her husband is cheating on her with her new best friend. She is thinking about an egg, and it is a metaphor for her burgeoning self-awareness: "It's almost pulsing; Sally is afraid of it. As she looks it darkens: rose-red, crimson. This is something the story left out, Sally thinks: the egg is alive, and one day it will hatch. But what will come out of it?" (1058).

One wouldn't have expected from the outset that the story could culminate in this sense of existential crisis and possibility for Sally. Initially, she appears to be utterly in control, not only of her own life but that of her husband as well. If we expect dawning self-awareness from any character, surely it will happen to Ed. Sally is happily married to Ed, who is a divorcee. She is reducing a sauce for that evening's dinner party, reflecting generously on her husband's stupidity: "For it must be admitted: Sally is in love with Ed because of his stupidity, his monumental and almost energetic stupidity" (1041).

The story is narrated in the third person, but we identify with Sally's perspective. So it comes as a bit of a surprise to discover, a few pages into the story, that Ed is a heart surgeon. Ah, we may say, he's a doctor, but he has no emotional intelligence. It's ironic, we may go on to reflect, that people who are so smart can be simultaneously so stupid. That he is a "heart man" (1043) only makes the irony all the richer. Well done, Margaret.

Atwood isn't finished with us yet. In fact, she's only getting started. It's true that Ed may be a man of abstracting, objectifying rationality. He is an adept with the machinery in his lab, and seems not to notice or to care about what his wife is thinking or feeling. On holidays, he wins ruthlessly at Monopoly, then takes himself off to bed. He is twice-divorced. Yet he's not quite as oblivious to the advances of other women, who are constantly asking him to listen to their heart at dinner parties, as his wife thinks. Then there's the revelation that he is probably having it off with Sally's friend Marylynn: "Ed is standing too close to her, and as Sally comes up behind them she sees his left arm, held close to his side, the back of it pressed against Marylynn, her shimmering upper thigh, her ass to be exact" (1056–57). This evidence can be made to support the case that Ed, with his male way of ordering the world, is both the problem and the focus of Atwood's artistic achievement in the story. Yet she offers more.

Eventually, the evidence accumulates to the point of excess and explodes our confidence in Sally. In the story's final paragraph we realize, as she herself seems to, that she is on the cusp of an unprecedented level of *self*-knowledge. Now we reread the evidence. It turns out that she's a good candidate, at least according to the caricatures of the mid-'80s, for the stupidity she assigns to her husband. In keeping with the typical male caricatures of the time, she is guilty of little ditzy accidents, like burning toast and letting the Jacuzzi overflow, and the silly vanity of wanting an expensive table for an alcove because she's trying to evoke the scene of an old coffee ad. It turns out her friend is more witty about Ed's stupidity than she is: "Marylynn is even better than Sally at concocting formulations for Ed's particular brand of stupidity, which can irritate Sally" (1043). Like a bored, rich, suburban housewife, she tries a lot of different jobs, but they all end up "leading nowhere" (1044); and she takes night courses "to coincide with the evenings Ed isn't in" (1051). Her weaknesses, however conventional, strain our sympathy for her.

In the night course she is in at the present, "Forms of Narrative Fiction," she has been set the task of transposing the Bluebeard story from a particular point of view. Atwood at one and the same time critiques canonical literature, mimics male expectations, and engages in gynocriticism. The Bluebeard story exists in different versions. Atwood references the famous one by Charles Perrault, who wrote down a large series of tales for the pleasure of King Louis XIV. If feminist criticism has helped to call into question the arbitrary stability of the canon, it has also drawn attention to the arbitrariness of privileging stories that were written down, usually by men, and taken out of their *material* context, their oral, embodied, communal, folk environment.

Not only does Atwood make this male practice visible, she inserts Sally (and herself) into the story tradition. Both on the level of the character Sally, responding to the instruction of her female teacher Bertha, and on the thinly veiled meta-level of transposing the tale herself, Atwood adds layers of female artistic commentary on what has been a male preserve. What she does in this story is really quite ingenious.

Sally has been aware for a long time, from before the beginning of this course, that she spends too much time thinking about Ed: "She knows she thinks about Ed too much. She knows she should stop. She knows she shouldn't ask 'Do you still love me?' in the plaintive tone that sets even her own teeth on edge" (1051). Nonetheless, she decides to write the story from the egg's perspective because Ed is the egg: "(Ed isn't the Bluebeard: Ed is the egg. Ed Egg, blank and pristine and lovely. Stupid too. Boiled, probably. Sally smiles fondly.)" (1054).

Part of the reason that Sally thinks Ed is stupid is that she cannot access what's going on inside of him: "In her inner world is Ed, like a doll within a Russian wooden doll, and in Ed is Ed's inner world, which she can't get at" (1051). Atwood is gifted at conveying the sense, almost worthy of Greek tragedy, of the fear, sadness, and despair that Sally's life portends: "'Sally, Sally,' he says, and everything proceeds as usual; except for the dread that seeps into things, the most ordinary things, such as rearranging the chairs and changing the burnt-out lightbulbs" (1051).

Sally does not realize that it is not Ed that she does not understand, but herself. She lacks *self*-knowledge, what the Greeks enjoin in the saying "Know thyself." Using the metric she applies to Ed, this is the height of her "stupidity." As her true situation dawns on us as readers, we sympathize so ardently with her in her predicament that we dare not call it stupidity. It's more like the human condition, this vulnerability to the lies and predations of others whom we have trusted. With *Ed* in mind, Sally asks, "But how can there be a story from the egg's point of view, if the egg is so closed and unaware?" (1055). This is the challenge that Atwood sets *herself*, and to which she rises magnificently, with *Sally* as her subject.

Atwood takes on all the clichés from the early 1980s of Canadian upper middle-class wealth and female *ennui* and concentrates them in a figure she invites the reader to think of as stupid. Atwood jams the machinery of the day by presenting a character her reader can "see through," someone whom we may condescendingly pity, or with whom we might become impatient for their lack of self-awareness. The very way in which the author fulfils expectations and elicits emotional responses makes visible the logic of abstraction and manipulation that male discourse has mastered and with which the story's readers are complicit. We feel greatly for this character, both in spite and because of her flaws. In the end, Sally transcends even our valuations, whatever they may be. She is a pulsing, vibrant life, full of possibilities.

Underneath is a story and a subject matter rooted in oral tradition and popular history. This reality feeds the speculations of male-dominated literate culture, but is available for recovery and the expansion of female identities too.

Conclusion

Feminism puts pressure on "rationality" as betraying male assumptions and a male way of ordering the world. In so doing, it draws attention to massive oversights in the way literature has historically been conceived and who its practitioners and adepts are. One strategy it gives theorists (feminists and others too) is that of mimicry, which can have the effect of jamming male-shaped expectations and male categories. Whether or not Margaret Atwood was directly influenced by Irigaray's theorizing, her story "Bluebeard's Egg" plays with the then-conventional assumption that rationality is a male domain, and with the way male-centred expectations have shaped encounters with literature.

3

Rationality Is White

Introduction

If, for one set of critics and theorists, rationality is male, for another it's white. Or at least Anglo-American. This chapter is about the way racial assumptions shape culture, expectations, and ideas about the way things are. For critical race theorists, the prevailing approach to literary studies in the past has privileged white Anglo-American perspectives with effects similar to those confronted by feminist critics.

For critical race theorists, the dominant culture understood in racial terms assumes that it is disinterested and unbiased. It assumes that it proceeds according to the tenets of rationality. Yet its assumptions strangely line up with the way that the dominant culture thinks, and in the Western Anglo-American tradition of literary studies, that culture is decidedly white. With reference to issues of ethnicity or race, in the study of English literature one might say that rationality is white. Race theory puts pressure on concepts, terms, and categories that are associated with supposedly rational detachment and objectivity. An assumption of neutrality informs the following phraseology of Rivkin and Ryan: "Many ethnic studies scholars have begun to question the implicit assumptions that allow a white-dominated ethnic culture to present . . . ."[1] Whatever the *ethnic* culture may present, the fact that that culture is "white-dominated" skews its purposes with "implicit assumptions." "Whiteness," then, is a norm or a benchmark, presented as if stable, neutral, simply an objective point of reference.

Lisa Lowe's study of heterogeneity, hybridity, and multiplicity focuses on the very idea of ethnic homogeneity. It is one "that the dominant Anglo group fosters in order to dilute and, ultimately, destroy singular and

---

1. Rivkin and Ryan, *Literary Theory,* 961/1104.

different ethnic cultures."[2] The argument here is that the dominant group treats other groups as wholes and fails to recognize details that make people individual. For Lowe, this tendency can manifest itself even in the way that certain writers portray their own culture. She singles out Amy Tan for discussion, and this chapter will explore Tan's short story "Two Kinds" in terms of the issue that Lowe raises. The general point concerns all forms of critical race theory and is important to theory in general: namely, that what passes for rationality fails to account for particularities. The dominant passes for the universal.

Critical Race Theory

Rivkin and Ryan introduce the phrases "white-dominated ethnic culture" and "Anglo-American" as similar to one another, as describing an assumption about what can be taken for granted. "Anglo-American" refers to the heritage of white, English (British) influence upon and shaping of American culture. It also refers to an enduring assumed commonality in outlook between Americans and the English. Insofar as "Anglo-American" concerns a certain philosophical outlook and strongly suggests a north Atlantic geographical locale, the phrase can include the assumptions of some Canadians as well.

Rivkin and Ryan stress the fact (now becoming untrue) of "the Anglo-American majority's" status as a majority.[3] That dominant culture has historically figured various ethnic groups as its "others."[4] What the word "majority" connotes becomes clear in a telling descriptive phrase: "the mainstream culture defined and shaped by Anglo-American needs and concerns."[5] What one finds in "mainstream culture," especially as it concerns standards and assumptions to be taken for granted in the arts, has in fact been "defined and shaped" by a ruling group.

One key idea is virtually synonymous with rationality in the context of ethnicity and race: rationality is hegemonic. "Hegemony" entails the notion of a ruling group and the group it dominates. The basic meaning of the term is captured in the following phrase from Rivkin and Ryan: "a mainstream

---

2. Rivkin and Ryan, *Literary Theory*, 961/1104.
3. Rivkin and Ryan, *Literary Theory*, 959/1102.
4. Rivkin and Ryan, *Literary Theory*, 959/1102.
5. Rivkin and Ryan, *Literary Theory*, 960/1103.

that seems blissfully unaware of its own hegemony."[6] The majority or "mainstream" is not even aware of its own position of dominance. This term also captures the sense of *structuring* various social relations.

The three labels "white," "Anglo-American," and "hegemonic" come together in Rivkin and Ryan in a closing comment introducing critical race theory. This comment concerns the problem that needs to be overcome: "as the culture becomes less hegemonically white and Anglo, a different set of concerns will no doubt begin to emerge . . . ."[7] For now, these terms can concentrate the attention on what is otherwise taken for granted and serves as the basis for what is assumed to be rational inquiry.

Rivkin and Ryan write about ethnicity and race with reference in the first instance to the American situation and American history. This is a limitation of the text, of which they are undoubtedly aware. Regardless, they organize their introduction to critical race theory in terms of prevalent ethnic groups in the American context. They use this structuring principle to present various theoretical concepts and terms.

The four ethnic groups Rivkin and Ryan identify include: African Americans; Native Americans; Latino and Chicano people; and Asian Americans. They introduce key theoretical issues as part of their introduction to each of these four groups. Part of the theory of race concerns the *history* of its unfolding. Rivkin and Ryan note that African American literature was first in garnering attention, but that it made the writings of other ethnic groups more visible too.[8] The problem facing the literatures of ethnic groups other than the dominant one has been similar to that facing women's literature: the dominant group has not thought that other ethnicities were capable of producing literature worthy of the name! Within a framework of Anglo-American assumptions, the criteria used for such judgements have the appearance of objectivity and reasonableness. On the most superficial level, the study of literature in a university context gives the impression of the objective importance of what one studies. What one doesn't study is, by implication, less important. Yet the criteria for aesthetic judgement, in this setting as in others, turn out to be shot through with bias and self-interest.

In the case of Native American writings, that which has been undervalued includes "religious, mythic, and oral dimensions."[9] The rational has been

---

6. Rivkin and Ryan, *Literary Theory*, 962/1106.
7. Rivkin and Ryan, *Literary Theory*, 963/1106.
8. Rivkin and Ryan, *Literary Theory*, 963/1106.
9. Rivkin and Ryan, *Literary Theory*, 960/1103.

associated with what has been stabilized into written form; the oral suggests the ephemeral, the untrustworthy. Native American culture, however, cannot be reduced to its writings. Its oral traditions indicate the importance of local community and of living memory to the people. Here too one can see overlap with feminist concerns. For example, in writing "Bluebeard's Egg," Atwood helps to recover a folklore tradition that is submerged in male writings, which offer a form of abstraction.

Latino and Chicano criticism, meanwhile, has heightened awareness of borders, the creating of which involves rational abstraction and the exercise of power. In critical race theory, borders evince the arbitrary imposition of controls in the guise of neutrality, efficiency, and order. The topic of borders also lends itself to the exploration of differences in language and what counts as appropriate speech, what can be deemed to be sufficiently literary.

Finally, and perhaps most powerfully, Rivkin and Ryan discuss the reality of heterogeneity. They do so in the context of Asian-American writers, though this issue is very broadly applicable, both in critical race studies and beyond. A label like "Asian-American" cannot do justice to "the tremendous multiplicity"[10] within this supposedly unified group. Part of the diversity of what gets labelled "Asian-American" stems from the variety of historical circumstances that inform the experiences of those supposedly identifiable as a group. Significantly, the very notion of easily identified ethnic groups is fraught. It has implications even for the way the Rivkin and Ryan textbook introduction is laid out!

Paying attention to such an awkward situation will go hand-in-hand with an examination of language. A similar progression in the description of the history of feminism and the development of certain feminist positions has been observed. In that context, the word "constructivism" was enlisted to complicate how one approaches issues of identity and frameworks. We shall return to the massively important issue of the role of language in more detail in later chapters in this book. Lisa Lowe's emphasis on heterogeneity will help to prepare the way conceptually. Lowe also introduces a set of terms related to this key concept.

---

10. Rivkin and Ryan, *Literary Theory*, 961/1104.

Heterogeneity and Hegemonic Thinking

The introductory section of Lisa Lowe's essay "Heterogeneity, Hybridity, Multiplicity: Marking Asian American Differences" encapsulates some key vocabulary, an illustrative rhetorical move, and logic similar to Irigaray's. Furthermore, it too raises an anxiety-inducing political problem. The vocabulary and the core issue in this reading pervade literary theory!

In this essay, one encounters the Japanese terms *issei, nisei,* and *sansei*[11] at the outset. It's a strange rhetorical hook! The terms, however, which refer to people of different generations, introduce the predominance of generational thinking at an early stage of Asian-American studies. For Lisa Lowe, such thinking can help one identify hierarchical and hegemonic thinking. She is going to teach the reader how. Inter-generational conflict has proven to be a popular theme among Asian-American writers. Yet for Lowe, such a dominant form of storytelling itself masks a significant hegemonic practice.

Lowe spends considerable time on the portrayal of generational change in Asian-American literature;[12] it sets up her significant move. However, it is easy to miss her real concern because she starts with the presentation of *conflict*. That theme would seem to align with a concern for the problem of power, and so it does. Children from the younger generation have to work their way out from under the expectations of the older one. Lowe takes some time acquainting the reader with the details of such storytelling. Readers will readily recognize the importance of verticality as a concept linked to power and they may be deceived into thinking they are already in the theoretical thickets. As we saw last chapter, theory exposes rationality as power. Yet the reader simply looking for the theme of power as a sure sign of theorizing will be unprepared for what happens next. In tracking Lowe's development of the generational theme, one can fail to register how the latter theme reinforces certain other assumptions, namely an overly simplistic understanding of power dynamics.

Simply on the level of rhetorical analysis, even if one can report where Lowe ends up, it's good to be able to follow how she got there. Lowe offers a particularly trenchant remark that clearly establishes the change in emphasis she wants to see. Half-way through a long, involved paragraph in a section that already sounds like it is full of technical, theoretical jargon, Lowe writes the following: "However, I will argue that interpreting Asian American

---

11. Lowe, "Heterogeneity, Hybridity, Multiplicity," 1031, 1046n1.
12. Lowe, "Heterogeneity, Hybridity, Multiplicity," 1031–33.

culture exclusively in terms of the master narratives of generational conflict and filial relation essentializes Asian American culture, obscuring the particularities and incommensurabilities of class, gender, and national diversities among Asians."[13] In the original text, that quotation only takes us to a semi-colon, but there's already plenty there to work with!

It's easy for a reader to miss this sentence, simply because the paragraph in which it is embedded is so long. She deploys this rhetorical strategy to illustrate how *something else* can be going on in the midst of a situation that seems to be headed in a certain direction. The need to think differently about ethnic issues necessarily must happen within an existing discourse and set of assumptions. The length itself of the sentence, and the terminology it deploys, can be rather overwhelming: "master narratives," "essentializes," "obscuring," "particularities," "incommensurabilities," and "diversities." One might wish to pause here simply to take in the rhetorical feat. The language can be daunting, so much so that one might miss the one key word that signals a change in the argument: the word "However." Within the framework of the representation of family and generational narratives, Lowe has introduced a telling "However."

The first long clause to follow recapitulates what she has been saying about the theme of generations, introducing a useful term at the same time. The phrase "Master narratives" suggests the kinds of things that are said over and over again, so that they come to be expected and received unquestioningly. Such narratives come to be so embedded that they are taken as part of the very rationality that is thought to be neutral. The adjective "master," additionally, recalls the notions of power and implied violence encountered in the study of feminist theory. In this context, generational thinking is the master narrative.

What happens next represents the turn in her argument. The problem with the master narrative is that it "essentializes" and the act of essentializing has the effect of "obscuring." The word "essentializes" was also encountered in feminist theory. Let's leave it alone for now; it's a difficult word. What is obscured? Lowe goes to work on describing what gets lost when one essentializes. She refers to obscured "particularities" and "incommensurabilities." It may seem that the recognizable terms that follow, namely "class" and "gender," are the ones to seize upon. *As important as they are, the words "particularities" and "incommensurabilities" flag something even more basic.* They refer to realities that cannot simply be classified, abstracted, or lumped

---

13. Lowe, "Heterogeneity, Hybridity, Multiplicity," 1033.

together in a typical rational exercise. In the last phrase of the quotation, she adds a third term, "differences." It also appears in the essay's title. Particularities, incommensurabilities, differences: these are the things that are obscured. These are the details of a lived life. These are the things that are in danger of being lost whenever categories are created.

Now the meaning of the word "essentializes" becomes more clear and more powerful. To essentialize is to do the work of creating categories. "Essentializes" indicates an assumed unity, a forced wholeness, a hasty lumping of things together, identifying what matters most, an essence. The word "essentialize" is in important ways another way of referring to the work of rationality.

One might pause here for a little self-test. If the essay is about "heterogeneity, hybridity and multiplicity," with which terms in the quoted sentence are they aligned? To which are they opposed? These are all words that draw attention to unlikeness, to uniqueness. They are aligned with particularities, incommensurabilities, and differences. Lowe gives the reader here a half dozen absolutely central and key words that can help guide one to an important theoretical clearing. We'll necessarily return to all of these terms when we look at the work that has been done on language: they are key. The terms "heterogeneity," "hybridity," and "multiplicity" can be applied broadly. They will be encountered often, across different theories. Here, we see them in a usefully schematic context.

Having introduced a *vertical* concept, that of generations (and with it hierarchy and power relations), Lowe appeals to the terms "heterogeneity," "hybridity," and "multiplicity" to explode what one might think of as wholes. The wholes disperse in *horizontal* directions. Any one of the generations of Asian Americans, *issei, nisei, et cetera*, is itself not a whole, only to be thought of in relation to other generations. There are differences *between* Asian Americans of the *same* generation. This fact may seem obvious. Lowe's point, though, is that grouping all people of one generation together obscures the uniqueness of the people within the group. The act of grouping is an exercise of power or of complicity with existing power that is more subtle than intergenerational conflict. In the time in which she was writing, certain authors *not from the dominant class* were blind to it and were effectively blinding still others. Lowe discusses a story by Diana Chang to get at the importance of differences between people who have previously been treated as part of a unified whole. Lowe makes the claim that "Chang's story explores the 'ethnic' relationship between women *of the same generation*."[14]

In the following two paragraphs of Lowe's essay, phrasing associated with difference proliferates: "'messier'"; "a heterogeneous entity"; "different from, and other than"; "different distances"; "cultures as different as"; "unstable and changeable"; "complicated"; "quite heterogeneous and of discontinuous 'origins.'"[15] Effectively, what Lowe does is to take a vertical understanding of power relations and add a horizontal dimension to it.

If we think in terms of generations, we can conceive of the previous generation being above the next one on a descending timeline.

The various groupings, however, are not so tidily unified in this or any other structure. The phrase "heterogeneity, hybridity and multiplicity" opens up a *horizontal* diversity within any of the groups.

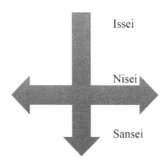

14. Lowe, "Heterogeneity, Hybridity, Multiplicity," 1033, emphasis mine
15. Lowe, "Heterogeneity, Hybridity, Multiplicity," 1034–35.

Any of the supposed groups is more, well, *heterogeneous* than was previously supposed. *This reckoning on horizontal complexity does not only apply to thinking about generations; it applies to any conception of groups, power, and suppression as a vertical relationship.*

While "hegemony" can be used very roughly to connote unfair power imbalances that ought to be redressed, such a rough understanding of the term fails to include the impulse to horizontal diversification. Within a hegemonic construction, even if one valorizes or makes visible a group that is in a lower position vertically, one is in danger of replicating or leaving unexamined the make-up of the group. The logic essentializes *all* the groups involved.

The issue that Lowe identifies is similar to the one identified by Irigaray. To contest male authority is to deploy an abstracting logic; it is to immerse oneself within a way of thinking that signals defeat *before one has even begun*. In critical race theory, to assume the identifiability and homogeneity of a group is similarly to accept or concede a power move before one has even begun. It is necessary to destabilize what is taken for granted as the so-called group's so-called identity, especially when that identity is foisted upon it from the outside. That's why Lowe can say that the ultimate aim of her argument is "to disrupt the current hegemonic relationship between 'dominant' and 'minority' positions."[16] The idea is not simply to defend minority groups over and against dominant ones, or to strive to invert them. Whatever else those minority positions may be, they are not homogeneous wholes. In the context of challenges facing Asian Americans, the aim is "to destabilize the dominant discursive construction and determination of Asian Americans as a homogeneous group."[17]

Nonetheless, and finally, Lowe recognizes a dilemma similar to the one that we observed provokes anxiety in feminism. There is a difficulty in speaking for any other, even sympathetically, and, simultaneously, a problem with remaining silent in the face of injustice. In both cases, the challenge is political. Lowe does not want simply to silence or thwart "those modes of argumentation that continue to uphold a politics based on ethnic 'identity.'"[18] She goes on to clarify the point rather emphatically: "I argue for the Asian American necessity—politically, intellectually, and personally—to organize,

---

16. Lowe, "Heterogeneity, Hybridity, Multiplicity," 1035.
17. Lowe, "Heterogeneity, Hybridity, Multiplicity," 1035.
18. Lowe, "Heterogeneity, Hybridity, Multiplicity," 1035.

resist, and theorize *as* Asian Americans."[19] In other words, she wants Asian Americans to work together as a group. She realizes that group identity is not altogether bad. The political necessity of solidarity comes under threat when one emphasizes "heterogeneity, hybridity and multiplicity" with the aim of disrupting identities. Lowe would seem to be acknowledging that it is always possible to divide what one has previously construed as a group or as a whole, but that it is not always expedient or appropriate to do so.

Generations and Heterogeneity in "Two Kinds"

In reading a story like Amy Tan's "Two Kinds," if one is thinking with Lisa Lowe then one should be alerted to its presentation of a generational conflict. Lowe writes, "In many Asian American novels, the question of the loss or transmission of the 'original' culture is frequently represented in a family narrative, figured as generational conflict between the Chinese-born first generation and the American-born second generation."[20] She goes on to place Tan in this tradition. We have seen that she expounds this theme to critique it.

It might be possible to disagree with the way Lowe reads Tan, but her short story "Two Kinds" certainly presents a generational conflict. In the story, a young second-generation Asian American woman is reflecting on her upbringing and the heavy-handed influence of her first-generation mother who sacrificed a great deal in journeying to America. Their battle centres on piano lessons. The mother wants the daughter to be like a child prodigy she sees on television. The daughter doesn't know what she wants, only that she has no intention of conforming to her mother's wishes. The story's basic structure fits a generational model pretty well.

Nonetheless, there's more that one can do with the story by deploying the reading strategy that Lowe helps to make available. The stronger the theory, the more widespread its applicability. One question that Lowe invites is whether we can find instances of heterogeneity, hybridity, and multiplicity in the presentation of a culture, *even if those examples are unintended by the author*. Amy Tan's story makes for compelling reading in this regard. Suddenly the lives of the narrator's mother *and almost invisible father* come into sharper focus as two lives lived in relation to one another in ways that remain obscure to the reader. Similarly, one wonders about the life story of the piano

19. Lowe, "Heterogeneity, Hybridity, Multiplicity," emphasis hers.
20. Lowe, "Heterogeneity, Hybridity, Multiplicity," 1033.

teacher to whom the mother sends the daughter. Though of the same generation as the mother, is his past as fraught? The protagonist's mother and that of the narrator's school friend clearly have entered into a social competition with one another of the sort that might seem familiar to us from the master narrative of generational conflict, but perhaps there is greater difference between the women than one is initially inclined (or invited) to think. Maybe the same diversity applies to the two girls who, in a generational narrative, might seem as undifferentiated as two pawns.

The protagonist herself may not be as unified as one assumes. The story presents her at one point in front of a mirror, confronting her uncertainty over who she is and who she wants to be, whether she can be her own person, and whether—either in caving in to her mother or in doing the exact opposite—she can escape the influence of her mother. At the end of the story, the image changes from a mirror to two pages of music. The sheets are meant to harmonize with one another, but the protagonist never saw the connection when she was younger. Tan suggests a wholeness and unity achieved over many years that a Lowe-inspired reading might want to continue to interrogate.

Conclusion

Critical race theory highlights the tendency in past Anglo-American literary studies to assume whiteness, and with it a neutrality and objectivity where other forces are at work. These forces begin to reveal themselves when one looks in historical perspective at what has counted as great literature and who wrote it. To think in terms of critical race theory is to recognize that notions like "beauty," "aesthetic," and "excellence" are shaped in part by the expectations and assumptions of a dominant group. Similarly, phenomena like orality and communal memory can reach us already with a certain baggage, as if they represented a less-than-rational way of looking at the world. Yet one begins to realize that the terms that one has used to define or to describe what counts as rational are themselves unstable. The notion of a whole of any kind very easily represents the overlooking of particularities and specificities. Critical race theory can draw one's attention to power in a general way. It can also do more. It can heighten one's awareness of issues of verticality *and* the need to exert horizontal pressure to expose plurality and multiplicity where a certain kind of rationality might assume unity and wholeness.

4

Rationality Is Repression

Introduction

If rationality for a feminist seems to be very male, and for a critical race theorist it is white, for a psychoanalytic critic rationality is repression. Here's an extended quotation from Rivkin and Ryan's introduction that summarizes the situation:

> That primary process of life is entirely irrational, and it cannot distinguish images and things, reasonable objects and unreasonable or socially unacceptable ones. It is the secondary processes of the mind, lodged in the ego and superego or conscience, that bring reason, order, logic, and social acceptability to the otherwise uncontrolled and potentially harmful realm of the biological drives. But, according to Freud, the drives of the unconscious, though repressed, can never be quelled entirely.[1]

As with the other two theories already examined, here too one can see the centrality of the question of rationality. In psychoanalysis, rationality is secondary to "biological drives." "Order," "logic," and "social acceptability" all have a family resemblance to "rationality." For Freud, the lot of them arise out of something more primordial.

The primary form of rational expression in contemporary society is science. Scientific discourse often presents itself as authoritative, definitive, and comprehensive. Yet Freudian psychoanalysis can be very effective at showing other factors, other dimensions, at play in the midst of earnest displays of rational control. The scene "There's nothing but chemistry here" from the opening season of *Breaking Bad* illustrates the desire

---

1. Rivkin and Ryan, *Literary Theory*, 391/569.

for a totalizing scientific explanation of reality that is simultaneously undermined by other forces.

This scene involves a flashback to a happier time for the central character Walter White, a time when he was a researcher. He and grad student Gretchen Schwartz are breaking down the components that make up the physical body and reach the point where they have accounted for 99.888042% of its composition. Walter observes that "We are .111958% shy." Gretchen says, "Supposedly that's everything." When Walter expresses dissatisfaction, she suggests, "What about the soul?"

Gretchen's question is naïve from two different perspectives. From a materialist point of view, the suggestion is naïve because there is no soul. The human animal is only bits of physical matter. Her suggestion is also naïve from a theological perspective, for the soul, like God, is not a reality to be measured: it cannot be restricted to science's canons of discoverability and provability. In philosophical language, to suppose that inquiry into the reality of the soul could be restricted in that way involves *a category mistake*. Being one-tenth of 1 percent shy of a complete accounting of matter in the body is not proof of the existence of anything. Whether scientifically or philosophically, we with our various techniques cannot exhaust the question of the possibility of the soul's existence. Like God, it can hide from our view. When materialists claim otherwise, they depend on principles or methods of their own devising, an inescapable framework. To make a claim about the universal applicability of their method they necessarily take a step of faith.

The makers of *Breaking Bad* get at this limitation in what follows. From his position at the chalkboard, Walter glances over his shoulder and chuckles, assuming Gretchen is joking. When she holds his gaze, he walks up to where she is seated, puts his arms on those of her chair, and leans in. We then see the scene from a perspective across the room, with a backdrop of the tall windows of the classroom giving onto a beautiful view of mountains and blue sky in the distance. With the figures silhouetted against the light, it looks like he is about to kiss her. "The soul?" he says. "There's nothing but chemistry here."[2]

No shit, Walter. The scene leaves open the question of what chemistry means, and whether Gretchen is probing to see if she has found her soulmate. It leaves open the question of whether chemistry can account for our experience of love or of beauty, whether the beauty of another

---

2. Penny, "What about the soul?" 1:00.

human being or of nature. (It also leaves open the question of whether they ripped each other's clothes off in the aftermath of this conversation.) At the moment, from the perspective of the camera, Walter appears to be oblivious to the beauty just outside the window and even to the glitter in Gretchen's eyes. In seeking to quash any metaphysical speculation on the part of his research assistant, he seems also to narrow the range of ways he can experience what the world offers.

Freud's claim puts extreme pressure on the idea of a pristine, disinterested, logical, orderly, rational faculty that allows one to have confidence in the objectivity of one's own thinking processes. Freud himself was a materialist, but he recognized that the dominant way of talking and explaining things in his day did not adequately account for the entirety of human experience. His argument was designed to shake to the core our confidence in ourselves as rational beings.

Freudian Psychoanalysis

Freud is telling us that *whatever* we are doing and thinking that may seem eminently reasonable to ourselves is a subterfuge to mask something else. It is a deception; we are self-deceived. What if this is true?

Freud's views have implications for an understanding of the self that took shape centuries earlier and is still dominant. The Viennese psychoanalyst challenged a view that appeared in a decisive way with a book by René Descartes written in 1641 called *Meditations on First Philosophy*. In order to understand this part of the story, we need to extend our timeline to encompass the intervening centuries. It must now include Descartes and the seventeenth century.

As we will see, Descartes gave modern philosophers a way of thinking about the self that privileged rationality. In fact, 1641 serves as a useful date for thinking about when north Atlantic cultures began to be *modern*. "Modern" is a term that can have many different meanings, and therefore can have various dates attached to it. For instance, students in literature and art may be familiar with modernism as a period of change and experimentation associated with the early twentieth century. Philosophically speaking, dating the modern era, dating *modernity*, from the mid-seventeenth century makes a lot of sense.

Psychoanalysis, then, gains traction in Western intellectual life for reasons that go back in time well before Freud and the appearance of his book *The Interpretation of Dreams* in 1900. Slowly but surely one can see a historical timeline developing and with it the sense of an unfolding historical narrative. If we take the time now to develop our timeline even further, we can place Descartes himself, materialism, and the development of the scientific revolution in a narrative context. This context will be a Western European one. Although readers of this book are now newly aware of different ethnic histories (thanks to critical race theory), and even though not all will share a Western background, the West plays an important part in this story and is the context in need of development here.

One might start the timeline again with a very simple line extending back in time to ancient Greece and Rome. In the West, the story of Christ plays a crucial role, so that for a while time itself was divided into BC (before Christ) and AD (*anno Domini*, the year of the Lord). The latter mimics the way Roman emperors began calendar time with the beginning of their own rule. In contemporary societies, *partly owing to a change of the controlling narrative,* BCE is commonly substituted for BC and CE for AD, but the events that mark the shift remain the same.

Ancient Greek and Roman Civs BC/BCE	Christianity AD/CE

Christianity grows and becomes the dominant form of belief and practice, so much so that people sometimes speak of Christendom—a Christian emperor, ruling a Christian empire, working in harmony with the Christian church. This religious unity was rocked first by a schism in 1053 between the Eastern and Western parts of the church, which produced the current division between Catholics (in the West) and Orthodox (in the East). In the West, it is further rocked by the Protestant Reformation. One does well to register the date of 1517, a year associated with the protestations of Martin Luther against the church to which he belonged. Part of the timeline therefore looks as follows:

RATIONALITY IS REPRESSION

Taken as a whole, this timeline stretching from antiquity to the present looks like this:

What happened after 1517? What happened between 1517 and 1641 that might be relevant to Descartes's writing of his book? Europe entered into a messy time of state and religious violence. Because the religion of Christianity played a pivotal role in European civilization, these battles had an enormous effect on whole countries and on all of Europe. Who had authority? What counted as authority? How should a society make the most basic decisions about justice, morality, and freedom?

René Descartes wrote his book to try to put the situation on a new footing. If he could provide the appropriate grounding, groups would no longer appeal to the Bible or the church or the Eucharist as a final "court of appeal" or point of reference. Instead, they would appeal to reason itself. It wasn't as though, previously, Christian thinkers had set reason aside, but they had complicated ways of talking about the relationship between faith and reason.[3] By the seventeenth century, their various formulations seemed not to be working. The door had been opened for conceiving authority differently.

How was one to appeal to reason itself? What was the basis of reason? Descartes came up with the formula, "*Cogito ergo sum*" ("I think, therefore I am"). The very fact that one could think was, for him, proof that one existed. It seemed that one could trust in the solidity of the "I." It became easier and easier to imagine everything—from thinking to doing science to acting politically: all aspects of our engagement with the world—as the activity of this basically stable and self-contained point of reference, the (modern) self.

We still think this way all the time. The animated movie *Inside Out* shows the inner workings of a young girl, Riley, in the midst of a difficult family move. The movie makes a profoundly philosophical assumption.

---

3. In fact, so too did Descartes. Henry, *La barbarie*, 23–36.

While all the interesting and tender investigations of Riley's emotional life are being played out, the whole story reinforces the conception of Riley's control center as a sphere. However connected "she" may be to other pods, and however important these connections may be to her overall health, the ultimate independence and solidity of one bubble at the center of its own reality is not questioned. It does not seem that this (apparent) reality is even something that *could* be questioned.

When one walks through the opening paragraph of Rivkin and Ryan's introduction to psychoanalysis, one sees that they begin with an allusion to the time of Descartes:

> A picture of the human mind as a unified whole that can achieve full awareness of itself has been central to Western thought since the seventeenth century. The "cogito" or thinking self defines our humanity and our civility, our difference from animals chained to blind nature and uncontrollable instincts.[4]

The reader is now better able to contextualize such phrases as "Western thought," "the seventeenth century," and of course the "thinking self." One does well to note as well the phrase "a unified whole." It has previously been encountered in discussions of essentialism. Here, the notion of a unified whole is brought together with full self-awareness or rational self-knowledge.

The editors then quickly introduce the concept of repression, specifically the repression of basic drives having to do with sexuality and violence:

> [Freud's] discovery was that the human mind contains a dimension that is only partially accessible to consciousness and then only through indirect means such as dreams or neurotic symptoms. The "unconscious," as he called it, is a repository of repressed desires, feelings, memories, and instinctual drives, many of which, according to Freud, have to do with sexuality and violence.[5]

It is tempting to reduce Freudian psychoanalysis to sex, but Freud is interested in violence too. For this influential European thinker, the human mind contains a dimension that is dominated by drives that elude rational control. As Rivkin and Ryan go on to observe, for him "our mental lives derive largely from biological drives."[6]

---

4. Rivkin and Ryan, *Literary Theory*, 389/567.
5. Rivkin and Ryan, *Literary Theory*, 389/567.
6. Rivkin and Ryan, *Literary Theory*, 389/567.

Those drives are more bizarre, more wild, more embarrassing than most of us would care to imagine, let alone admit. It's really important, whether one is a fan of science or of *Inside Out,* to try to imagine a world teeming with savagery underneath the seeming ordinariness of, say, activity in a library reading room, the blandness of people's choice of clothing, or a sonnet. For Freud, the whole edifice that we call "civilization" is a shit show contrived to cover up other things that are going on underneath. In fact, civilization itself comes to be defined as repression. Shakespeare, architecture, Mozart, *The Simpsons,* traffic lights, the Olympics, *Friends,* where you put your keys: it's all the manifestation in one way or another of what we individually and collectively keep repressed, transformed into supposedly socially (and personally) acceptable forms. What's really going on, derived from our material being, occurs in the realm of the unconscious. It is the activity of the Id.

One of the most basic manifestations of this reality, this doubleness, is the sense of it. Freud calls this sense "the uncanny." We will read him for ourselves by looking at his essay on the subject. Rivkin and Ryan introduce readers to other phenomena as well that suggest a seething reality underneath our civilized appearances. These include dreams, neuroses, and fetishes. Freud said dreams provide "the royal road to the unconscious" and it makes sense: the censor of our divided selves, the ego, is asleep. Asleep, but not dead. This is how Rivkin and Ryan describe the pivotal activity of dreaming:

> Unconscious wishes can find expression in dreams because dreams distort the unconscious material and make it appear different from itself and more acceptable to consciousness.[7]

In dreams, that which one cannot confront consciously through the activity of rational self-reflection becomes more apparent. Therapeutic psychoanalysis in part helps the analysand (the person being analyzed) to interpret their dreams as part of the process of coming to terms with their unconscious. Neuroses and fetishes function like dreams: they radiate clues about what is being repressed. Dreams, neuroses, and fetishes all provide subtle evidence of a truly overwhelming reality.

One of the great features of psychoanalysis is its broad applicability. The would-be theorist can quickly realize that one need not limit oneself to poems and plays to apply Freudian insights. If all of civilization is the

---

7. Rivkin and Ryan, *Literary Theory,* 568.

realm of repression, then all of civilization can be "read" in Freudian terms. All of our supposedly rational achievements, from the way we dress to our scientific achievements, invite analysis and redescription. *That's one of the great insights of theory generally: it is possible to redescribe cultural works.* The generalizability of ways of "reading" has contributed significantly to the transformation of many Departments of English into Departments of English and Cultural Studies.

Freud makes the impact he does as a reader of literature himself. Not only does he "inaugurate the critical genre"[8] with a reading of E. T. A. Hoffmann's story "The Sandman," he offers an influential interpretation of the story of Oedipus, a tale from ancient Greek literature. In the case of psychoanalysis, a popular and enduring form of contemporary theory quite obviously grows out of literature. It takes up ancient questions often asked in literary form. Those questions revolve around the status of rationality as a component of the human experience. To those who think of theory as a distraction from literary studies or as newfangled, the point needs to be stressed that the questions posed by theory and literature alike have been with us for a long time.

The Irrationality of the Uncanny

Freud's 1919 essay "The Uncanny," published nineteen years after *The Interpretation of Dreams,* combines numerous strategies. It includes a word study, a review of a leading theory, classicism, contemporary cultural criticism, remarkable rhetorical closure, and imaginative reach. Part of the essay's fame comes from how much it holds together.

The most important of Freud's strategies is the one deployed at the outset, repeated and developed in the second section of the essay. It concerns the status of rationality. Freud moves consideration of the "uncanny" out of the realm of knowledge. Rationality cannot access that which is most true about this sensation. Beginning in typical scholarly fashion, Freud cites a scientist named Jentsch as his intellectual interlocutor. He does so to stress the point that, for Jentsch, the uncanny is simply what is unfamiliar. Jentsch conceives of the uncanny in terms of what is known, giving it a place on that spectrum: "We are tempted to conclude that what is 'uncanny' is frightening precisely because it is *not* known and familiar,"

---

8. Rivkin and Ryan, *Literary Theory,* 568.

RATIONALITY IS REPRESSION

Freud writes.⁹ He adds, "On the whole, Jentsch did not get beyond this relation of the uncanny to the novel and unfamiliar."¹⁰

After a foray into a word study, he returns to Jentsch, and to this point. Jentsch associates thoughts of the uncanny with "'doubts'"¹¹ as to whether an object or animate reality is alive or not. The father of psychoanalysis goes on to quote Jentsch's emphasis on *uncertainty*, or the state of the reader's *knowledge* about given figures: "one of the most successful devices for easily creating uncanny effects is to leave the reader in uncertainty . . . .'"¹² Freud appreciates the attention Jentsch draws to the idea of the uncanny, as well as to Hoffmann, but he isn't satisfied with the construal of "uncanny" on offer. He wants to remove it from the realm of knowledge and rationality.

For Freud, the genuine phenomenon of uncanniness lies in the experience of substitution and of doubles. He retells Hoffmann's story in considerable detail to replace the notion of uncertainty with that of substitution. "There is no question, therefore, of any intellectual uncertainty here," he says in summary fashion.¹³ At that point, he explains the significance of all the references to the eyes he has highlighted. At that point, too, he folds in the Oedipus story: "The self-blinding of the mythical criminal, Oedipus, was simply a mitigated form of the punishment of castration—the only punishment that was adequate for him by the *lex talionis*."¹⁴

For Freud, uncanniness cannot be explained in rational terms. That is, for him, the issue is not one of greater or lesser degrees of knowing; for him, there is something else going on. Freud makes heavy appeal to the language of logic and reason at this point *in order to push away from it*: "We may try on *rationalistic* grounds to deny . . . and may *argue* . . . and may *argue*. . . . Indeed, we might go further . . . no other significance and no deeper *secret* than a *justifiable* dread *of this rational kind*."¹⁵ One can now see fully the importance of Jentsch's argument and the grounds on which Freud is putting it aside. He is not putting it aside because he disagrees with the amount of rationality Jentsch allows; he disagrees with the emphasis on rationality altogether.

9. Freud, "The Uncanny," 418/593, emphasis his.
10. Freud, "The Uncanny," 418/593.
11. Freud, "The Uncanny," 421/597.
12. Freud, "The Uncanny," 421/597.
13. Freud, "The Uncanny," 424/599.
14. Freud, "The Uncanny," 424/599.
15. Freud, "The Uncanny," 424/599, emphasis mine.

Distancing himself from Jentsch allows Freud to put in place a very different kind of "explanation": "this view does not account adequately for the substitutive relation between the eye and the male organ."[16] Freud has just made his move, and what follows has brilliant internal consistency. One should not make the mistake of thinking, however, that he is interested in satisfying anyone's intellectual curiosity. He is tracing the energies of life, the drives, the forces that lie below the surface. He is engaging in an act of imagination rather than providing a rationalistic explanation, which is why I put the word "explanation" in quotation marks at the start of this paragraph. As we have seen with Irigaray and with Lowe, were he to make a linear argument, he would be appealing to a framework that is secondary. He would remain within a rational way of construing things, and therefore within in the realm of repression.

Childhood is a site of primal energies, as well as a time when a battle between primal and policing forces give shape to our repressions. Freud talks about childhood in terms of forces; he does not attempt to offer a rationalistic construal of this strange time of life. He appeals to this realm to pursue two different points: he wants to gain access to the theme of the double; and he wants to make a sweeping analysis of the whole of Western civilization. These two impulses appear together in his summary of Otto Rank's treatment of the double.

Rank's treatment of the double likewise resembles both Irigaray's logic as to why feminists ought to prefer mimicry to argument and Lisa Lowe's argument why it is not enough simply to strive for a counter-hegemony. There's a paradox at work in Rank's analysis. The double has to do with "belief in the soul and the fear of death."[17] Inventing a double is meant as "a preservation against extinction"; it springs from "the soil of unbounded self-love."[18] The double will survive death. For Rank, and for Freud, this invented double later becomes, paradoxically, *a reminder of the very thing it was invented to ward off*, death! Freud writes, "From having been an assurance of immortality, he becomes the ghastly harbinger of death."[19] The very phenomenon of the double, then, is uncanny: the very thing simultaneously means its opposite. In its primal manifestation in childhood, the double declares the all-pervading reality of death.

16. Freud, "The Uncanny," 424/599.
17. Freud, "The Uncanny," 425/601.
18. Freud, "The Uncanny," 425/601.
19. Freud, "The Uncanny," 425/601.

RATIONALITY IS REPRESSION

Freud is making a second move here too, one easily missed. It appears in what seems like a throw-away line: "Such ideas," he writes, "have sprung from the soil of unbounded self-love, from the primary narcissism which holds sway in the mind of the child *as in that of primitive man*."[20] Freud reads history as if it were a developing person. If this book has been gesturing to a timeline, Freud has one in mind too! He will return to it in a later paragraph: "It would seem as though each one of us has been through a phase of individual development corresponding to that animistic stage in primitive men . . . ."[21]

What Freud wants from this second point about the uncanny is to rescue modern humanity from archaic beliefs. This argument is at least as important as any therapeutic benefit for individual patients. Well, for him, being released from childish beliefs *is* therapeutic! "Our analysis of instances of the uncanny has led us back to the old, animistic conception of the universe which was characterized by the idea that the world was peopled with the spirits of humane narcissistic overestimation of subjective mental processes . . . ."[22] Freud is giving us his version of the argument, commonplace in his time,[23] that humanity created gods to explain the unknown: "all those other figments of the imagination with which man . . . strove to withstand the inexorable laws of reality."[24]

Whether in our lives as individuals, or collectively as a developing species, the doubles that we have created are preserved in "traces" and "can be reactivated."[25] This experience, had in many different forms, carries with it an "uncanny effect."[26] Freud explained how a word, *heimlich*, could come to have opposite meanings. In this way, he vivified the phenomenon of repression. More importantly, where both repression and the uncanny are concerned, he moved the conversation away from a basis in rationality. He left rationality itself to be the principal manifestation of the repression of all that is more primal and animalistic within us.

---

20. Freud, "The Uncanny," 425/601, emphasis mine.
21. Freud, "The Uncanny," 428-29/604.
22. Freud, "The Uncanny," 428/604.
23. It may have been common, but it was not the only view. Lucien Lévy-Bruhl and Émile Durkheim offered a very different explanation of how the primitive mind worked. For an illuminating discussion, see Owen Barfield, *Saving the Appearances*, 28–35.
24. Freud, "The Uncanny," 428/604.
25. Freud, "The Uncanny," 429/604.
26. Freud, "The Uncanny," 427/602.

Rationality and Repression in "The Use of Force"

Whether intentionally or not, the early-and-mid-twentieth-century American poet, writer, and practicing physician William Carlos Williams masterfully enters into Freudian dynamics in his short story "The Use of Force." Sex and violence are both in play. So too is the questionable value of rationality and the dubious status of a doctor as a paragon of reason.

In this short story, first published in 1938, a concerned couple have asked their local doctor to make a house call to diagnose their ailing daughter during an outbreak of diphtheria. The setting evokes comparisons with a quaint picture by Norman Rockwell depicting a kindly male doctor interacting indulgently with a precocious young girl.

Norman Rockwell, *Doctor and Doll* (1929).
Illustration provided by Curtis Licensing.

Williams frames the story in terms of the solidity of life in middle America. It exudes a sensibleness centred on the wise, friendly doctor who has ample expertise in handling the health needs of his community, even when they face an unusual threat like that of diphtheria. This world, however, breaks down over the course of the story.

The doctor is presented as a symbol of authority and rationality. As a medical practitioner, he has extensive training. He has scientific authority on matters of bodily health; in the era in which the story is set, "doctor knows best"; his say-so over what is happening in the body matters more than the opinion or perspective of anyone else in the room. Relative to this (male) figure of authority, the parents are abject. The mother presents an image far from that of calm rationality. She is beside herself for having to ask the doctor to make a house call: "a big, startled looking woman, very clean and apologetic."[27] The father occupies a position of deference and implied incompetence. With his daughter in his lap, he cannot get up to greet the doctor as he comes into the kitchen, who reassures him "not to bother." The doctor's professional condescension consolidates his position of pre-eminence. Later, the doctor will ask for the father's assistance, but the latter will prove to be unhelpful.

The doctor, meanwhile, through whose eyes we experience the story, assesses the situation judiciously. He presents the events in an even tone that conveys his approach to the situation on the day. As readers, we trust him. He has responded to the parents' call and, without making a fuss, enters the heart of their home, the kitchen. He puts on his "best professional manner" and the mother endorses him as "such a nice man." Later we'll learn that he wears glasses, another symbol of intellectual authority, as is sight itself. He makes detached, rational observations as an outsider: "I could see that they were all very nervous. . . . They weren't telling me more than they had to, it was up to me to tell them." When he looks at the girl, he can read her symptoms: "her face was flushed, she was breathing rapidly, and I realized that she had a high fever." He makes the swift diagnosis of the professional who has seen it all before.

Yet other less reassuring details are already emerging as well. Before we learn about the symptoms the girl is presenting, the good doctor tells us that she "was fairly eating me up." Something within him is already responding to her on an emotional, if not animalistic, level. He goes on to report that she was "an unusually attractive little thing" with "magnificent blonde hair,

---

27. Williams, "The Use of Force," np.

in profusion." He compares her to pictures of children in leaflets and papers. One wonders if he has a private stash of them. He has a public excuse for what happens next, but the situation is descending to a level where the language of rationality reads like a poor covering.

Meeting initial resistance, he approaches the girl a second time to get a throat sample, and she reacts "suddenly." He uses animal imagery to describe her actions and then addresses her in a new, adult tone: "Look here ..." and "You're old enough to understand what I'm saying." He notes her faster breathing, then admits that he has entered into a "battle" with her. He rationalizes his actions: "I had to do it." A few sentences later, he confesses, "I had already fallen in love with the savage brat." The parents and the trappings of civilization are falling away to reveal primal forces: "she surely rose to magnificent heights of insane fury . . . ."

The father is alternately unhelpful ("till I wanted to kill him") and complicit in what reads like a sublimated episode of sexual aggression. The girl splinters a wooden tongue depressor with her teeth, causing her mouth to bleed, but the doctor doesn't desist, again rationalizing his actions as a public good:

> . . . feeling that I must get a diagnosis now or never I went at it again. But the worst of it was that I too had got beyond reason. I could have torn the child apart in my own fury and enjoyed it. It was a pleasure to attack her. My face was burning with it.

The doctor-narrator admits that he had got "beyond reason." His statement comes across not so much as an admission but as yet another rationalization. He appeals yet again to a bulwark of rational acceptability, this time "social necessity." Then, however, he says starkly: "But a blind fury, a feeling of adult shame, bred of a longing for muscular release are the operatives." The phrase "muscular release" places the source of motivation at the opposite end of the spectrum from rationality, in the directives of a body acting of its own accord. He overpowers her in "a final unreasoning assault."

The doctor emerges intact from the episode within a culture that justifies his actions to the parents and to himself, but for the reader (whether one in the 1930s or the twenty-first century) it's too late. Williams has pulled back the curtain of an apparently sensible and necessary interaction between community members in a society gathered reasonably around a clearly known common good. He has exposed forces of desire and violence behind a cultural façade.

Conclusion

In psychoanalysis, rationality is a mask. It hides the forces that actually control us and constitute our being. These forces are grounded in physical reality. While psychoanalysis no longer looks very scientific to many people, Freud shares with many modern scientists a commitment to materialism. He does not, however, trust blindly in rationality. Aware of the foibles of human nature and the deep mysteries of human behavior, he develops a system of explanation involving numerous brilliant, imaginative moves. Probably as much as any other modern theory or system of thought, Freudian psychoanalysis undermines an unwarranted confidence in the idea of the self as autonomous and reliable.

Freud developed his theory through a careful consideration of literary resources, and has had a significant influence on the development of creative writing and literary criticism in the twentieth century. He remains a force in literary theory, both in his own right and for the influence he has had on other theorists who have attacked rationality from various directions.

5

Conclusion to Section I

Some readers may have been expecting the appearance of the word "ideology" for a while. This word encapsulates the phenomenon of how, historically, one group could think that something is neutral when in fact it serves their interests. That something could be an action, a policy, a monument, a list of authors to be studied, degree requirements, any number of things. The following definition of "ideology" encompasses and summarizes many of the observations that have been made in the first section of this book:

> The concept "ideology" reflects the one discovery which emerged from political conflict, namely, that ruling groups can in their thinking become so intensively interest-bound to a situation that they are simply no longer able to see certain facts which would undermine their sense of domination. There is implicit in the word "ideology" the insight that in certain situations the collective unconscious of certain groups obscures the real condition of society both to itself and to others and thereby stabilizes it.[1]

In the context of feminism, "ruling groups" can be taken as men. Men are in a ruling position and, from a feminist perspective, "are simply no longer able to see certain facts that would undermine their sense of domination." In the context of critical race theory, especially as applied in an Anglo-American context, the ruling group can be understood as white people.

In a certain context, the word "ideology" connotes class warfare and therefore has a political application of a particular kind. In that context, some might marginalize feminism and critical race theory as social rather than political issues. When one emphasizes how groups simply cannot "see certain facts which would undermine their sense of domination,"

---

1. Mannheim, *Ideology and Utopia*, 40.

then one can more easily set the phenomenon in a wider context. Issues of power and therefore politics apply directly to feminist and racial concerns, as they do class conflict.

In this description, psychoanalysis also plays a role. The author of this definition appeals to the role of the unconscious: "in certain situations the collective unconscious of certain groups obscures the real condition of society both to itself and to others." This Freudian word further draws attention to the sense of there being forces at play shaping our perceptions of which we are not cognizant.

The word "ideology" represents a powerful claim. It goes beyond the notion that ruling groups know what they are doing and wilfully choose to ignore "certain facts." "Ideology" captures the notion that the ruling group *cannot even see* certain realities. If the capacity at least to "see" reality is the basis of rational deliberation, then "ideology" is another word that directly challenges the common understanding of the nature of rationality. It likewise stares down the assumption that "rationality" refers to something that actually exists. In a world dominated by choice—acts of the will predicated on deliberation—"ideology" strikes at the core of many people's self-understanding.

Most can relate to the questions that arise in feminism, critical race theory, and psychoanalysis. They belong to our world and make sense to many people. They may be theories, but they aren't *just* theoretical. They aren't *just* academic. Issues of gender and race, especially, have contemporary relevance. Freudian psychoanalysis also still has enough cultural currency to help make theory accessible. The aim of this section has been to introduce theory in a way that shows that its central concern is not altogether foreign. That concern—that rationality masks things—is mainstream in Western cultures.

Because it isn't *directly* related to the hot button issues of cultural politics, perhaps psychoanalysis especially can help readers at the present time. It can help one appreciate the ethos that marks theory generally without pressing one's buttons. Freud clearly distrusts reason. It is hopefully pretty obvious that in the textbook explanations, in the theoretical readings, and in the literary readings as well, the interrogation of reason is a common theme.

To recognize the severe critique of reason is to grasp *the* central issue in literary theory. It is to get beyond (but not to downplay) a deluge of strange terminology and European names. Undergraduate students in the arts and newcomers to theory are sometimes asked to wield these names and terms without their appreciating what, fundamentally, is at stake. To recognize the critique of rationality is to take hold of a ribbon that can guide one through the labyrinth of theory, and through courses in various disciplines that apply it.

Nevertheless, it is strange and unnerving to imagine one's own situation in this regard: that when one is attempting to be rational, one can never entirely account for that which hides itself from one. Rationality as an activity in a neutral environment accessible to all on equal terms is nothing of the kind. It is one thing to appreciate the unmasking of bias and the attack on a "rationality" that serves male or white interests; it is one thing to recognize a general inclination not to acknowledge forces that we hardly control; it is one thing to see the problem *out there*, in a set of issues labelled one way or another. *It is quite another thing to come to terms with the notion that situatedness and limitation marks us here and now, however sensitive and well-meaning we may be as readers and interpreters.* The conundrum concerns not only the flagged issues of the day; the problem concerns the very basis of what it means to be rational or to claim to think critically. If Freud is right, and if the other theorists are right as well, then unconscious bias is not something simply to be overcome. Neutrality is not a goal to be achieved. Philosophically, one may not yet have come to terms with the implications of situatedness.

An exercise one might undertake to acclimatize oneself to the environment of theory is to write about one of the poems or short stories examined in the previous chapters, but to do so from a perspective different from the one already applied to it. The task is straightforward enough; the results it produces might surprise you! To look at "The Use of Force" from a feminist rather than a psychoanalytical point of view will produce insights that haven't already come to light in the discussion above. To look at "Bluebeard's Egg" through the lens of critical race theory poses certain different challenges.

The exercise fails, however, if unaccompanied by the recognition that we cannot change perspectives *at will* and *entirely*. The exercise is just that, an exercise. We are not perspective-free beings who put on perspectives at will and otherwise apprehend reality without one. Nor is it appropriate to imagine ourselves ever perfectly amalgamating all perspectives into one. To imagine that we could do so either individually or as a society is to pursue a fantasy. It is difficult to inhabit one's finitude, one's lived situation. The question is, where does that leave us as readers, interpreters, and human beings?

False Problems: Towards the Recovery of Rationality

6

Introduction to Section II

On Not Overcoming

The subhead for an opinion piece in the Canadian trade magazine *University Affairs* unwittingly bespeaks a contemporary intellectual misunderstanding: "Taking steps to ensure that conscious and unconscious bias do not play a role in hiring and promotion . . . ."[1] It is not possible for any of us to overcome not only our conscious *but also our unconscious* bias. There is no titanic act of the will or simple application of good intentions that can achieve that goal. There seems to be not even a minimal understanding in this quotation of what Freud means by the unconscious and what political theory has extrapolated from his insights (and not his alone).

Contemporary north Atlantic cultures still need to wrestle with the idea represented by the notion of the unconscious. One can in no way achieve perfect self-knowledge, ensure freedom from bias, or make good on the desire to control our environment. The unconscious bias is always *our own*. It belongs to those who would "ensure" freedom from conscious and unconscious bias *in the very process of "achieving" such a position of freedom*. A certain conception of freedom is simply unobtainable and inhuman.

Like the writer of the editorial in *University Affairs,* those encountering theory for the first time sometimes might think they just need to work harder and that now, thanks to their new theorizing abilities, they can. Ideology can seem like it's somebody else's problem. For example, it's easy to think that "ideology" is the blinder of the individual who identifies him- or herself not merely as culturally but as personally religious. One might think that they need to overcome their ideology in order to thrive at university.

1. Timmons, "Equal Opportunities," np.

This view represents a misunderstanding of the situation that theory would have us grasp. Each of us construes rationality in a way that is shaped by the narrative that we inhabit. The view that rationality is cold, neutral, detached, and objectivizing belongs to a particular, historical way of thinking about the world.

For the Greeks, the notion that we actually control our own situation and destiny is called *hubris*. It's what goes before a fall. Tragedy looms precisely when Oedipus takes action with the best of intentions. (In his case, he wanted to avoid a horrible prophecy that he would kill his father and sleep with his mother. The action that he took, running away from those whom he did not realize were his adoptive parents, precipitated his tragedy.) A popular and very modern discourse of untrammeled freedom perpetuates the illusion that one can somehow get behind one's situatedness, one's very human finitude. One cannot. Being human involves something different. We must collectively allow ourselves to be deeply affected by awareness of our limitations. We must feel deeply the difficulties to which the Greeks long ago drew attention. A questioning of the very notion of rationality has accompanied the Western intellectual tradition ever since. One need not look far to find such awareness in other traditions as well.

The implications of the critique of rationality are quite daunting. Feminism, critical race theory, and psychoanalysis represent a stance in literary and cultural theory generally. That position is that claims to rationality mask something else that is actually going on. The textbook writers Rivkin and Ryan clearly and consistently state that what is purported to be universal in fact represents interests. They believe that any gesturing towards essences is misguided at best and always pernicious. The theorizing of Lisa Lowe shows the importance of concepts like "heterogeneity, hybridity, and multiplicity." *All mainstream theories challenge what we think we know about rationality.* They all confront a related set of terms: universals, truth, wholeness.

Hidden Dimensions

In some ways, this attack is very salutary. In Greek fashion, it challenges *hubris*, overweening confidence in reason, science, or technology. It critiques the pretensions to God-like comprehensiveness of knowledge and the capacity for overcoming limits that mark the modern project of trusting solely in reason and in human capacities. The period in which these ambitions take hold is known as the Enlightenment. One might also say that they characterize *modernity* more generally. Theory in some ways challenges modernity itself; in some ways it challenges *hubris*.

The cure, however, may be worse than the disease. It involves accepting something like a constitutive desire that can never be satisfied, or a condition that looks to self-creation but not to truth. For many, it involves recognizing violence as primordial and reality itself as ultimately meaningless.

Yet for others, the critique of rationality as it has come to be understood releases other understandings. The critique itself is necessary and legitimate, but the implications as propounded by mainstream theory have been one-sided. To appreciate the contemporary environment, mainstream theory will be explored further, especially in terms of its approach to language. However, an alternative approach to the implications of this critique introduces nuances and possibilities that otherwise remain obscure. At an introductory level, these variations encourage the reader to continue to explore the essential critique of rationality without feeling that they must commit themselves to abandoning the Western intellectual tradition. Rationality, especially the modern scientific construal of it, will be kept under scrutiny. A different narrative direction, however, can be explored.

In the next two chapters five readings will be considered; their potential implications will then be explored in a series of poems dating from the Middle Ages to the present time. A different sort of text will also be engaged to underscore the point about theory's reach beyond "literary works" narrowly understood.

7

Rationality Is Judgement

Introduction

This chapter challenges the notion that rationality comes into its own with the exercise of critical judgement. Such an understanding privileges the notions of distance, observational objectivity, and emotional detachment. The writers to be considered are far from overturning the main tradition of Western philosophy, however. They all in their own way strive to recover a rich understanding of rationality, one that does not attempt to isolate it from values and from the imagination.

Initially, the reader is confronted with a succinct but powerful claim for the role of the emotions, especially love, in the reasoning process. John Macmurray provides a quite beautiful and memorable contrast between two ways of conceiving the role of the senses in our knowing. Terry Eagleton, one of the most influential teachers of literary theory, takes up the theme of the relationship between knowing and loving. He helps the reader to see how literature has long considered rationality as related to love and desire. Eagleton also encourages the reader to reconsider the relationship between "facts and values." Scientific modernity works hard to keep these notions apart from one another. Eagleton transposes their meaning in terms of the relationship between love and reason.

The second half of the chapter encourages the interpreter to reconsider their relationship to works of art, to the past, and to the task of interpretation generally. Rather than supposing that the task is first of all to establish a critical distance whereby one might exercise skills in judgement, Hans-Georg Gadamer would have us recognize how the past already informs us. It is literally already part of us. The task is not to look *at* works and writers of the past but to exercise the imagination and look *with* them. Gadamer believes that rationality beckons us, and that there is no contradiction between interpretation, on the one hand, and seeking to discover resonances between past, present, and future horizons, on the other.

Reason *and* Emotion, Facts *and* Values

In a short exposition, John Macmurray establishes a useful contrast between two ways of knowing. This contrast can help one to appreciate the limitations of a certain approach to rationality while deepening one's sense of its power when redescribed in relation to love and to sensual pleasure. In this moving excerpt from his book *Reason and Emotion,* he contrasts *knowing-about* with *knowing the thing itself.* The pictures that he paints are compelling in their clarity and obviousness. I will quote him at length because part of the joy of reading Macmurray is simply to dwell in the different realities that he presents. We find ourselves admitting, Yes, that's how I spend too much of my time each and every day. That's how I approach the world around me! and then resonating with the alternative, recognizing that he has articulated something that we very much believe and know to be true, even if we do not always live according to our best insights and desires. Macmurray *gives us permission* to believe that hope and love can have a place in the way we conduct ourselves as interpretive and rational beings.

In the first instance, he describes a kind of knowing *for the sake of using;* it is a knowing for *our* purposes:

> Now, there are two distinct ways in which we can employ our senses; a thin and narrow way, and a full and complete way. The thin way comes from restricting the senses to the use we can make of them for practical purposes. We have a marvellous capacity for failing to notice what stares us in the face, if it is not immediately related to the purpose and interest that dominates our minds. If the interest is narrowly practical, what we perceive in the world will be a narrow range of utilizable facts.[1]

Macmurray is here presenting one way of thinking about rationality. It is altogether possible to think that rationality means organizing one's day and one's environment according to the agenda that one has set for oneself. This can have the appearance of objectivity, but in fact one might simply fail to notice or feel the need to account for that which is not "immediately related to the purpose and interest that dominates our minds." In fact, at

---

1. Macmurray, *Reason and Emotion,* 21.

this point the reader might well be thinking, What's the alternative? How would one even describe it?

Macmurray continues in this vein:

> In the first case our senses are specialized instruments for achieving definite, prescribed purposes. We use our eyes to look for something we have lost, to gain information about how we can cross a busy street, and so on. We use our ears to gain information that will be useful to us in furthering our ends, and become deaf to everything else. Sense-awareness, in that case, is only a means to an end. Its value for us lies not in the awareness itself but in the things it enables us to do. We may call this the practical or scientific use of the senses, in which they provide, on the theoretical side, data which can be elaborated by thought into a general theory; and on the practical side, facts which we must take into account in planning for action and in acting.[2]

This way of approaching this world reaches us in a very practical sense, and for that reason Macmurray initially takes his examples from day-to-day life. Yet it describes the scientific outlook as well, in which the furthering of our ends sets the agenda. The notion of value does enter into this way of thinking, but only as value "for us." As we shall see with Eagleton, a scientist need not be dominated by this "thin" way of being. Macmurray, however, diagnoses a modern tendency.

The other way of using the senses involves knowing something *for its own sake*, knowing some thing because one *loves* that thing. Surely what he says rings true:

> But when we use our senses just to become aware of what is around us, for the sake of the awareness itself, we use them in a different and fuller way. We can look at things for the joy of seeing them; we can listen to the sounds of the world because it is good to hear them, without any ulterior motive or special purpose. In that case, we look at things not because we want to use them but because we want to see them. We touch things because we want to feel them. Sensitive awareness becomes then a life in itself with an intrinsic value of its own which we maintain and develop for its own sake, because it is a way of living, perhaps the very essence of all living. When we use our senses in this way we come alive in them, as it were, and this opens up a whole new world of possibility.[3]

2. Macmurray, *Reason and Emotion*, 21.
3. Macmurray, *Reason and Emotion*, 21–22.

It seems to me that Macmurray is describing the *holiness* of things and an attitude of reverence towards them. Yet it does not seem incongruous to assign the notion of rationality to such an attitude and active awareness. Macmurray is giving a vision of the capacity to escape oneself, to avoid reducing reality to one's own agenda, but instead to take delight in reality on its own terms. Such an achievement sounds like the attainment of objectivity. Paradoxically, though, it is achieved through entering into knowing with a sense of devotion, submission, and openness to joy. *Value* has a place in this understanding, and it is no longer value "for us," but rather a recognition of "life in itself with an intrinsic value of its own."

This is how Macmurray continues:

> We see and hear and feel things that we never noticed before, and find ourselves taking delight in their existence. We find ourselves living in our senses for love's sake, because the essence of love lies in this. . . . When you love anything, you want to fill your consciousness with it. You want to affirm its existence. You feel that it is good that it should be in the world and be what it is . . . . In fact, you are appreciating and enjoying it for itself, and that is all that you want.[4]

What a gorgeous description! Not only does it ring true, it gives us permission to love what we do and to trust the goodness of what we do. Even if we do not live like this all the time, Macmurray gives one something to aspire to in their intellectual life—a life that is not divorced from their moral and personal life.

A caricature of rationality—as sterile, detached, involving a view from nowhere—is still rightly under assault. The notion of objectivity, of rationality, being proposed here is bound up with *love*. Love may redeem reason itself. Love may turn out to be present in rationality all along.

Terry Eagleton is a Marxist critic who undertook to explain literary theory to a wide readership in the 1980s with his *Introduction to Literary Theory*, the most popular book on the subject ever written. That book was instrumental in the development of theory as a subject for undergraduate English majors back in the 1980s, partly because he writes so clearly, and partly because he is so funny. Eagleton has also contributed actively to theory with his own version of political criticism.

In a book he wrote some twenty years later called *After Theory*, he revisits the topic of theory in a general way and in it draws attention to

---

4. Macmurray, *Reason and Emotion*, 22.

rationality's relationship to love. For him, politics is relevant to both. It may even be a word that heals the splitting implied in words like "facts" and "values," "reason" and "emotion." The title *After Theory* bears comment. Once, when I was chair of my department and had to do such things, I looked over the syllabus of a senior colleague who had quite the reputation as our resident *avant garde* postmodernist. He had a line about the book in his course overview, but mistakenly referred to it as *Against Theory*. Clearly, he hadn't read the book, but the putative title fitted the narrative that he wanted to tell: that in some quarters there was a backlash against theory.

In *After Theory*, Eagleton isn't against theory at all. Anyone who reads as far as the second paragraph will know this:

> Those to whom the title of this book suggests that "theory" is now over, and that we can all relievedly return to an age of pre-theoretical innocence, are in for a disappointment. There can be no going back to an age when it was enough to pronounce Keats delectable or Milton a doughty spirit. It is not as though the whole project was a ghastly mistake on which some merciful soul has now blown the whistle . . . .[5]

Eagleton's concern is rather that prevailing trends in theory have pernicious implications stemming from what he identifies as an exaggerated attack on rationality and the notion of truth. One long passage that concludes a chapter entitled "Truth, Virtue and Objectivity" is very stirring. The venerable theorist says something counterintuitive when he writes that "objectivity is a political affair."[6] What can he mean? Isn't objectivity scientific and detached? Isn't politics messy, fluid, and driven by self-interest? Aren't objectivity and politics opposites?

One has already seen that scientific detachment does not necessarily yield the best understanding of a given subject matter. Typically, though, one is invited to think that if something cannot be approached in a spirit scientific objectivity, then it's subjective. Eagleton challenges that opposition. To call the political objective is to reclaim both the word "objectivity" and the political as the sphere in which it might be realized. He invites the reader to *imagine* their way into what this conjunction might look like.

From here, Eagleton directly confronts the notion of detachment. Objectivity, he says, "lies very close to love."[7] Having convictions—recog-

---

5. Eagleton, *After Theory*, 1–2.
6. Eagleton, *After Theory*, 131.
7. Eagleton, *After Theory*, 131.

nizing that one does not stand in some neutral space, a self-awareness in agreement with one of theory's main tenets—does not bar a person from being objective. Having convictions is very different from egoism. It enables, as he says, "a certain self-forgetful attentiveness."[8] His phrasing hints at what Macmurray also describes.

Like Macmurray, Eagleton paradoxically conjoins an inward receptivity and assurance with an outward gaze. One of the ways that love applies to the dynamics of exercising rationality rests in the following: knowing that one is loved enables self-forgetful attentiveness. Security is a condition of achieving objectivity: "If one is loved or trusted in return, it is largely this which gives one the self-confidence to forget about oneself, a perilous matter otherwise."[9] He links love and objectivity (or rationality) in another way too. It is our passion for a subject that enables us to persevere: "Knowledge needs to be disciplined, judicious, meticulous, self-critical, discriminating and so on, so that nobody without some sort of virtue could write a great history of the boll weevil or come up with a stunning scientific discovery."[10] I have heard many scientists affirm such a sentiment. Unfortunately, the recognition does not commonly reach the level of methodological self-understanding.

For most contemporary literary and cultural theorists, disinterestedness is the last word in naiveté. Eagleton agrees with them in acknowledging that we are always situated and need to recognize our limitations—that's theoretically sophisticated enough. Yet he avers that acknowledging that one occupies a position is the very thing that enables one to be politically consequential: one is in a position from which one can work to make life better for more people. Eagleton is building upon a theoretical insight into the problems *with a certain construal of rationality*—an understanding he shares—to advance a very different argument. His line of reasoning has its roots in Aristotle,[11] one of the leading figures in the philosophical tradition that mainstream theory disavows.

With Aristotle, Eagleton is challenging the notion that facts and values are separable. For Eagleton, "the modern age drives a wedge between . . . fact and value."[12] The words themselves have come to have connota-

---

8. Eagleton, *After Theory*, 131.
9. Eagleton, *After Theory*, 131.
10. Eagleton, *After Theory*, 132–33.
11. Eagleton, *After Theory*, 134.
12. Eagleton, *After Theory*, 132.

tions that make them seem very different things. In the hands of thinkers like Macmurray and Eagleton, though, facts and values are intimately connected to one another. Without values, facts remain obscured. The tendency is to think that because someone is involved or has convictions, that they are unreliable, prejudiced even, and unable to ascertain the truth of a situation. On this assumption, one tacitly, if not explicitly, privileges knowing-about over knowing. Yet one can easily see the difference between someone who knows about something in an external way and someone whose knowledge of a subject matter brims over in passionate engagement, and the superiority of the latter. We all have the experience of recognizing the authenticity and authority of loving attention to detail for its own sake in the one whose knowing we trust and admire.

Before Alienation and Judgement

Hans-Georg Gadamer's essay "The Universality of the Hermeneutical Problem" provides a more formal introduction to the theory of interpretation called radical or philosophical hermeneutics. I would argue, though, that with Macmurray and Eagleton we have already been exploring its characteristics. The word "hermeneutics" is, in one sense, synonymous with literary theory because the term gestures towards interpretation. As shall become clear, however, Gadamer finds in it a rich and radical meaning. Reading Macmurray and Eagleton helps to prepare the ground for a productive reading of Gadamer. The notion of overcoming the fact/value split—a split Eagleton equates with "the modern age"—is useful; so too is the distinction between *knowing* and *knowing about*.

Gadamer establishes the context for his comments in the opening paragraph of this essay, where he mentions science twice early on and technology further down. For Gadamer, the question is "how our natural view of the world—the experience of the world that we have as we simply live out our lives—is related to the unassailable and anonymous authority that confronts us in the pronouncements of science."[13] I don't think Gadamer necessarily adopts a sardonic tone in his use of the word "unassailable" (well, maybe), but he probably does in calling its authority "anonymous." This is pretty severe language. He associates science with something "unassailable," like a bank vault, and with cold, impersonal "anonymous authority." It "confronts us" and makes uncompromising "pronouncements." All of this

13. Gadamer, "Universality," 3.

is in contrast with "our natural view of the world" and with our "experience of the world." Gadamer would have his reader be mindful of and open to their experience of the world.

In the same paragraph, he contrasts our awareness of "orders of our being" that "simply demand our respect"[14] with the "world of technology" that "the sciences place at our disposal."[15] Gadamer plays a little trick on us here, for now it seems that it's the "orders of being," not science itself, that are stony and recalcitrant, while science is busy putting technology at our "disposal." Gadamer would have us remember that our natural experience of the world involves becoming aware of limits and recognizing its otherness. These are part of the learning process, whatever science may pronounce.

He returns to science as a point of contrast (and context) throughout the essay. He warns us that the goal is not "to develop a kind of antiscience."[16] Rather, he would have us see that *science's "methodological abstraction" is encompassed by a "hermeneutical dimension."*[17] In other words, hermeneutical issues are bigger and of more fundamental importance than questions of method. They belong to an enlarged understanding of rationality itself. Preoccupation with method suggests the prior acceptance of an abstraction. As an example, Gadamer would have his readers see that a favorite activity of science, "the so-called random experiment,"[18] hides the decisive role of *imagination* in asking penetrating research questions: "It is imagination that is the decisive function of the scholar."[19] He makes no distinction between the scientist and the literary or cultural critic in this regard: both exercise their imaginations when they are working at their best.

If rationality is under attack in philosophical hermeneutics, we might say that, for this theory, rationality is judgement. By judgement, Gadamer means the modern, scientific habit of stepping back from one's situation to assess it critically, distrusting imaginative engagement. One does not do this only when one is doing science; rather, a scientific approach has pervaded our learning in many other areas as well. For Gadamer, before judgement comes into play something else is always happening first, and

---

14. Gadamer, "Universality," 4.
15. Gadamer, "Universality," 3.
16. Gadamer, "Universality," 10.
17. Gadamer, "Universality," 11.
18. Gadamer, "Universality," 12.
19. Gadamer, "Universality," 12.

one does not have the freedom to step back, at least not in the first instance. Something more compelling has already happened.

Gadamer makes his argument that something has already occurred before the exercising of judgement with reference to three topics or situations. It's tricky on a cursory reading of this essay to spot all three, because at the outset he mentions only two: "I would like to start from two experiences of alienation," he writes.[20] A few pages later, however, he finds himself wanting to establish a "contrast" to "these examples" of alienation, but immediately finds he needs to make a further clarification. That leads him to the third situation to be considered.

For Gadamer, "alienation" means the assumption that we are separated or set apart from what we are studying. In the first instance, he identifies this assumption as being at work in our experience of art. In the case of art, "this whole world of experience becomes alienated into an object of aesthetic judgment."[21] That's a bad thing. Initially, however, this isn't the way art reaches us or has functioned in societies. In ancient religious cultures, art wasn't produced for our detached assessment. Gadamer makes his point in the form of a twofold rhetorical question, but his intention is clear:

> Is it not true that when a work of art has seized us it no longer leaves us the freedom to push it away from us once again and to accept or reject it on our own terms? And is it not also true that these artistic creations, which come down through the millennia, were not created for such aesthetic acceptance or rejection?[22]

The notion of an encroachment on our freedom might naturally make some readers bristle, but his point is that something more real, more engaging is going on when art seizes us. The question of our position of judgement (and the implied freedom that accompanies it) is secondary: "No artist of the religiously vital cultures of the past ever produced his work of art with any other intention than that his creation should be received in terms of what it says and presents."[23] The recognition that a work of art *is* a work of art is *secondary* to the fact that it makes an "immediate truth claim."[24]

This is bracing. Gadamer is in effect saying that the message of art reaches us before we have time to become sophisticated and push it away

20. Gadamer, "Universality," 4.
21. Gadamer, "Universality," 4.
22. Gadamer, "Universality," 4.
23. Gadamer, "Universality," 4–5.
24. Gadamer, "Universality," 5.

from ourselves, which we do supposedly to make an aesthetic judgement upon it. "I like that. Oh, I don't like *that*. See what she does with her brushwork here?" Blah, blah, blah. The more primordial reality is that we are connected to the artwork and to the artist.

Gadamer makes this same point with reference to history. We experience history as alienation. He refers to the modern study of history as "the noble and slowly perfected art of holding ourselves at a critical distance."[25] One must be careful. The German is playing with us here. "Noble and slowly perfected" sounds good, but it's in service of achieving "critical distance." He draws on Nietzsche, whom we will encounter in the third section of the book, to say that, as with art, we don't actually practice "historical distancing" but rather have an "immediate will to shape things."[26] When we practice detachment, we note only insignificant details, howsoever technical those details may be. When someone writes great history, something different happens: "the great productive achievements of scholarship always preserve something magic of immediately mirroring the present in the past and the past in the present."[27] Real history involves immediacy and connectedness. It involves the historian in her or his own situatedness. Far from trying to flee oneself in the name of a certain kind of rationality— i.e., detached observation—genuine knowing involves engagement of one's imagination, of one's own self, and of one's own circumstances. There is a parallel here to the paradox described by Macmurray and by Eagleton, in which love enables one to know properly.

From these two examples, Gadamer wants to generalize and he wants to use the word "hermeneutics," because he is interested in how interpretation actually happens. This turn in the discussion causes him to ponder a third situation where alienation is privileged. He finds that he must pull the word "hermeneutics" away from Friedrich Schleiermacher, an early nineteenth-century figure, for whom it means "the art of avoiding misunderstanding."[28] In this area, Schleiermacher represents both "the modern age," as Eagleton calls it, and the scientific emphasis on achieving critical distance.

---

25. Gadamer, "Universality," 5.
26. Gadamer, "Universality," 5.
27. Gadamer, "Universality," 6.
28. Gadamer, "Universality," 7.

Let's just pause to remind ourselves of our timeline. The early nineteenth century finds us in a time of consolidation of the principles of the Enlightenment.

Gadamer wants to rehabilitate the word "hermeneutics" because Schleiermacher's definition already presumes alienation, which Gadamer is unwilling to grant. He refers to "I and thou" as another formulation that some take to imply separation, when in fact it points to connectedness and commonality: "there is neither the I nor the thou as isolated, substantial realities. I may say 'thou' and I may refer to myself over against a thou, but a common understanding always *precedes* these situations."[29] He wants again to affirm and to draw attention to that *antecedent* shared reality, now figured as "a common understanding."

From here, Gadamer makes the startling move of recovering the pre-Enlightenment meaning of the word "prejudice." Understood *positively,* pre-judice refers to that which reaches us before we suppose we can step back from it in critical judgement. Properly understood, or at least, understood without the coloring of the modern age, pre-judices—the things that reach us before we assert ourselves to exercise judgement upon them—are the "conditions whereby we experience something."[30] To understand something is literally "to stand under" it, that is, to be in a position of submission or deference or receptivity to it, rather than one of manipulation, control, and possession. This does not at all imply that we cannot learn or receive a new perspective. The meaning of prejudice that becomes standard in the modern age is not in direct battle with the earlier meaning. Rather, the modern version of the word hides a commonality that makes meaningful dialogue and genuine growth possible.

Gadamer goes on to describe how we learn on the basis of our commonality. Here the role of the imagination really comes into its own. He talks about the importance of asking productive questions. Asking a good question, he insists, is a matter of the imagination. He enlists Socrates as an exemplary thinker precisely because of his creative questioning:

29. Gadamer, "Universality," 7, emphasis mine.
30. Gadamer, "Universality," 9.

> As a student of Plato, I particularly love those scenes in which Socrates gets into a dispute with the Sophist virtuosi and drives them to despair by his questions. Eventually they can endure his questions no longer and claim for themselves the apparently preferable role of the questioner. And what happens? They can think of nothing at all to ask. Nothing at all occurs to them that is worthwhile going into and trying to answer.[31]

The Sophists don't know how to ask good questions. They are not motivated by deep human questions welling up from within them, arising from their own humanity. The Sophists were, in fact, early rhetoricians who reduced language to the status of a tool. Gadamer, like Macmurray, critiques a preoccupation with utility.

The discussion of imaginative questioning brings the reader to a very significant juncture in Gadamer's overall argument. If one wants to be in dialogue with an artist—a poet, a painter, or some other figure from the past—the idea is not to look *at* them to try to figure out what they meant. The idea is to look *with* them. What is one looking *at*? One is looking in the direction of a subject matter that concerns both the interpreter and the artist being read or encountered. Interpretation, then, is not some direct confrontation with a figure from the past, but involves a third element, the subject matter itself. Discovering what that subject matter might be requires the use of the imagination.

As a professor, I have made the poetry of Geoffrey Chaucer (c. 1342–1400) my area of specialization. For Gadamer, I am only able to connect with Chaucer meaningfully as I bring to bear the questions that are already important to me. At some level, both Chaucer and I are asking questions of a common subject matter. I connect with him properly as I make his question (of the subject matter) my own, whether that question be the threat of tyranny, the nature of justice, why we laugh, or some other matter.

Here's how a commentator on Gadamer puts it:

> The dialogical character of interpretation is subverted when the interpreter concentrates on the other person as such rather than on the subject matter—when he looks *at* the other person, as it were, rather than *with* him at what the other attempts to communicate. . . . The interpreter must recover and make his own, then, not the personality or the worldview of the author, but the fundamental concern that motivates the text—the question that it seeks to answer and that it poses again and again to its

---

31. Gadamer, "Universality," 13.

interpreters. This process of grasping the question posed by the text [leads to the openness of a genuine conversation] only when the interpreter is provoked by the subject matter to *question further* in the direction it indicates.[32]

The interpreter is trying to reconcile his or her own question with the "fundamental concern" that motivates the text. The aim is not to have an encounter with the worldview of the author, nor is it to recover her or his original intention. Paradoxically, an encounter with the author *can* occur, but only as the interpreter truly pursues the subject matter for her- or himself. Interpretation involves being drawn on by the subject matter, what Plato calls the *logos*.

Conclusion

While affirming the rightness of critiquing rationality, this chapter has opened up ways of thinking about rationality positively. These ways are bound up with love, hope, and imagination. Counterintuitively, the very things that "the modern age" came to believe characterize intellectual inquiry—detachment, critical distance—make it harder to practice. Genuine rationality, including the possibility of objectivity and disinterestedness, depends on one's wholehearted involvement. To recognize this paradox can inspire in us a more vulnerable and imaginative engagement of the past, of art, and of others.

---

32. Linge, "Introduction," xx–xxi, emphases his.

8

Rationality Is Verification

Introduction

Like the titles of all the previous chapters, this one too redescribes rationality in a way that problematizes the concept. The last chapter observed that radical hermeneutics attacks a deformed version of rationality that gives pride of place to judgement; this one extends the hermeneutical critique to the notion of verification. Seeking to prove or to verify does not sufficiently account for what rationality involves. As a once popular book on the nature of intellectual creativity puts it, "provability is a weaker notion than truth."[1] Yet this chapter, like the last, resists overthrowing rationality and supposing that rationality necessarily masks something more sinister. This chapter continues the effort made in the last one to reclaim and to rehabilitate rationality.

Paul Ricoeur extends Gadamer's ideas and brings them more directly into contact with poetry. Ricoeur makes explicit the argument that to critique one form of rationality (he uses the word "obliterate"!) is not to abandon rationality altogether. Quite to the contrary, it encourages one to imagine reality in a different way, one in which the notion of connection before alienation figures prominently, and to adjust one's descriptive language accordingly. The second reading to be examined continues in this vein, drawing particular attention to the role of metaphor in poetry. For Rowan Williams, the nature of metaphor tells us something important that is relevant beyond the realm of literature alone.

The rest of the chapter returns to poetry and other artistic "texts." In all of these works, a theme emerges that depends on the ideas developed in

1. Hofstadter, *Gödel, Escher, Bach,* 19.

the last chapter and this one. They all insist on the importance of heterogeneity while affirming a great fullness and wholeness.

Hermeneutics and Poetics

At a pivotal point in his argument, Paul Ricoeur makes a transition from the analysis of sacred (biblical) texts along theological lines to that of secular works along philosophical ones. While respecting the differences between kinds of texts and ways of approaching them, he wants to suggest that something rather similar happens in both sorts of disciplines and in all forms of interpretation. The word "revelation" is relevant throughout. One might recall that in chapter 1 Jack Myers, writing about making poetry, also drew attention to this charged word. Reading Ricoeur reminds us that we have unfinished business with poetry.

Ricoeur writes, "I have not introduced the category of poetics heretofore . . . ."[2] This seemingly transitional remark comes shortly after he has made a reference to Gadamer. That reference alerts the reader to expect some commonality between the two thinkers. So too may the word "hermeneutic" in their essay titles. I suppose, while I'm at it, I'll just point out that in the paragraph just before he turns to the category of poetics, Ricoeur refers to the horizon or the intention of the author. He writes that "what is finally to be understood in a text is not the author or his presumed intention . . . but rather the sort of world intended beyond the text as its reference."[3] This statement might remind us of where we left things off with Gadamer. There we were learning that one doesn't want to look *at* the author, but *with* him or her in the direction of the subject matter that concerns both the reader and the author. The phrase "subject matter" is roughly synonymous with Ricoeur's phrase "the sort of world intended beyond the text."

Ricoeur helps the reader and interpreter rethink how one encounters ordinary reality. What appears ordinary may not be so, and seemingly rational ways of describing it may not be satisfactory. Ricoeur's agenda aligns with what has been observed in other chapters. From "The Outlaw" to "The Uncanny," art and theory shake us out of habitual ways of perceiving reality. One might conclude, with many theorists, that rationality itself is only ever a cover for self-interest or irrational forces. Like Gadamer, Eagleton, and Macmurray, Ricoeur accepts the critique of what is commonly accepted as

2. Ricoeur, "Towards a Hermeneutic," 100.
3. Ricoeur, "Towards a Hermeneutic," 100.

rationality, especially in the scientific modern world. Like them too, he extends that critique in his own way. However, he too also refuses to abandon rationality. Rather, he too enlarges the vision of what rationality can be.

In introducing the term "poetics," Ricoeur's first goal is simply that the reader not get hung up on distinguishing poetry as a form of literature from prose or drama. He is going to use the word "poetic" to describe a way of looking at the world, not to distinguish one literary form from another. Understanding how he is using the term poetics can itself unlock what he is doing in this reading.

Ricoeur then introduces the phrase "referential function." This weighty phrase will preoccupy him in the ensuing paragraphs. The first thing he wants to say is that poetry does not have a referential function. We very often use language like a tool so that we can do things like order coffee, talk about a movie, explain our actions, and generally get through the day. Scientists likewise use language as if it were a mathematical tool as they try to describe reality precisely or share their methods.

Ricoeur doesn't think we only approach reality and use language in an ordinary or a scientific way. The various genres that make up poetics do something different. He writes that they "exercise a referential function that differs from the descriptive referential function of ordinary language and above all of scientific discourse."[4] Ricoeur is distinguishing poetics from the *use* of language to achieve either ordinary or scientific ends.

Ricoeur wants to make sure that we understand what poetic language does to ordinary ways of talking and thinking: "the poetic function points to the obliterating of the ordinary referential function."[5] "Obliterating" is a strong word. Ricoeur clearly does not think that ordinary life and science account for all that language can do. He ends this short paragraph by saying flatly, "[Poetic discourse] does not directly augment our knowledge of objects."[6] Poetic discourse is not simply something we *use*. At this point, Ricoeur is making a good old-fashioned defense of the arts as distinctive, but at what cost? Is he merely saying that poetic language is, well, useless?

If poetry doesn't augment our knowledge of objects, what good is it? A parent might say, What good is an English degree *in the real world*? A scientist might refuse to take it seriously for anything that matters, skeptical of the capacity of poetics to foster any sort of rigorous thinking. A standard

---

4. Ricoeur, "Towards a Hermeneutic," 100.
5. Ricoeur, "Towards a Hermeneutic," 100.
6. Ricoeur, "Towards a Hermeneutic," 101.

artsy answer to such expressions of doubt has been to say that the arts and sciences concern themselves with different realities. Another is to say that, in the arts, one learns about what artists and aesthetes think about the arts; one learns that the arts are *reflexive*. (For example, Shakespeare is being at least partly reflexive when he says "All the world's a stage.") One might say that the arts don't concern themselves with any reality outside of themselves. Ricoeur is getting at such notions when he says, at the start of the next paragraph, "From here it is only a short step to saying that in poetry language turns back on itself to celebrate itself."[7]

Ricoeur isn't happy with this option. He perceives a problem with the either/or logic: that either poetic language does what other language does, or it turns back on itself. Ricoeur thinks that poetry concerns reality outside of itself. He essentially asks the same question as Eagleton: what is meant by objectivity? Look, he says, it's a *scientific* assumption to say "empirical knowledge is objective knowledge because it is verifiable."[8] Truth, or objective knowledge, or rationality is not necessarily a matter of proving things, of statements being "verifiable." In the rest of that paragraph, he defends a kind of referential function different from what is ordinarily expected, *but a referential function nonetheless*. In other words, poetic discourse refers to something. It has something to do with the real world:

> Too often, we do not notice that we uncritically accept a certain concept of truth defined as adequation to real objects and as submitted to a criterion of empirical verification. That language in its poetic function abolishes the type of reference characteristic of such descriptive discourse, and along with it the reign of truth as adequation and the very definition of truth in terms of verification, is not to be doubted. The question is whether this suspension or abolition of a referential function of the first degree is not the negative condition for the liberating of a more primitive, more originary referential function, which may be called a second order reference only because discourse whose function is descriptive has usurped the first rank in daily life and has been supported in this regard by modern science.[9]

---

7. Ricoeur, "Towards a Hermeneutic," 101.
8. Ricoeur, "Towards a Hermeneutic," 101.
9. Ricoeur, "Towards a Hermeneutic," 101.

The gist of this quotation is clear: Ricoeur is defending poetry as having something to do with the real world. The task that remains is to unpack his logic and his moves in this sequence of three sentences.

Perhaps the first step is to notice the repeated use of the word "adequation." In this context, it refers to the notion of a word, a painting, a mathematical formula, or any other representation matching what we think we see or know when we apprehend something. Adequation is a synonym for "referential function" in the sense of the ordinary or scientific uses of language. A second difficulty concerns the middle sentence, which begins "That language . . . ." Ricoeur is not here specifying one language as opposed to another. He is saying something along the lines of, "That I am coming for dinner is not to be doubted." That poetic discourse obliterates the referential function of ordinary or scientific language is not to be doubted. Finally, he troubles himself with phrases like "first degree," "second order," and "first rank" because he wants to defend poetics as having a referential function. He is saying that, in fact, there's nothing secondary about a poetic way of looking at the world. The problem is that we've got so used to starting with a scientific way of describing reality that we think that any other way must be secondary. That assumption bedevils the modern age, just as the fact/value split does.

To summarize this important paragraph, Ricoeur is saying, Yes, poetics "abolishes" a *certain kind* of referential function, but it liberates *a different one*, one that has been "usurped" by modern science.

Yet how can that be? How could it be that the modern respect for science and the understanding of rationality that accompanies it need to be "obliterated"? The answer comes at the start of the next paragraph. Ricoeur opens the reader up to a different way of thinking about the very nature of reality: "My deepest conviction is that poetic language alone restores to us that participation-in or belonging-to an order of things which precedes our capacity to oppose ourselves to things taken as objects opposed to a subject."[10] Along with all the other commentators in these two chapters, Ricoeur thinks that the idea of "distance" between oneself and reality—"our capacity to oppose ourselves to things"—falsifies the actual situation in important respects.

Poetic language, in whatever form it takes, suggests an alternative to thinking about reality in terms of subjects with objects placed before them. Ricoeur, like Macmurray, Eagleton, and Gadamer, is challenging

---

10. Ricoeur, "Towards a Hermeneutic," 101.

the presumption of thinking first of all in terms of subjects opposed to objects. In Ricoeur's vision of the real, art or poetry "redescribes reality so well known that it is taken for granted."[11]

Ricoeur enlists Aristotle's support for the view that art affirms a referential function that is more than imitation. Mimesis has come to mean just that: imitation or realism, like a nineteenth-century novel or a life-like picture by Norman Rockwell. As Aristotle understood the term, mimesis does not mean "slavish imitation, or a copy, or mirror-image, but a transposition or metamorphosis."[12] Richard Kearney, who studied under Ricoeur, also emphasizes this idea:

> When Aristotle defines *mimesis* in his *Poetics* as the "imitation of an action," he means a creative redescription of the world *such that hidden patterns and hitherto unexplored meanings can unfold.* . . . It has little or nothing to do with the old naturalist conviction that art simply holds up a mirror to nature.[13]

Reality is richer and deeper than one can know, and a sense of that depth is revealed through poetic discourse.

Instead of verification or proof, Ricoeur suggests that what one gets through poetics is "manifestation."[14] He goes on to say that "what shows itself is in each instance a proposed world, a world I may inhabit and wherein I can project my ownmost possibilities."[15] That sounds to me like "participation in" or "belonging to" the order of things, Ricoeur's earlier description of the nature of reality. Poetics enhances the sense of the revelatory nature of reality—"what shows itself"—and of the possibility of flourishing in a world that only reveals itself when entered into imaginatively. Somehow the possibilities apply to the "I" as well, an I at once responding to something given—something I may "inhabit"—and exerting itself creatively, poetically, if you will. The idea is not to prove things, but to flourish, to have freedom, to resonate with what is. Rationality isn't dissolved in poetry and one isn't left to make things up for oneself, but neither can it be said to take the form of detached objectivity and vaunt itself over everything else. Ricoeur offers a deep affirmation of a world that is knowable. That

---

11. Ricoeur, "Towards a Hermeneutic," 102.
12. Ricoeur, "Towards a Hermeneutic," 102.
13. Kearney, *On Stories,* 12, emphasis mine.
14. Ricoeur, "Towards a Hermeneutic," 102.
15. Ricoeur, "Towards a Hermeneutic," 102.

knowable world, however, is not given to us to manipulate, nor ought one ever to suppose that one could exhaust its meaning.

Poetry, Textuality, and the Actuality That Is There

A short excerpt from a book on art by Rowan Williams, himself a poet and also a former Archbishop of Canterbury, contributes to the major themes in hermeneutics explored here. It too challenges conventional ways of knowing and seeing while affirming rationality and its role in artistic creativity. I start at the very end of a section of *Grace and Necessity*, where Williams recounts a story about T. S. Eliot's interaction with a student. The exchange illustrates the important point that *art plays an irreplaceable role in the description of reality*.

Eliot's point is that poetry does not simply restate something that could be said in other terms:

> When asked by an undergraduate what he meant by "Lady, three white leopards sat under a juniper tree," he famously replied, "Lady, three white leopards sat under a juniper tree."[16]

In this conviction, the poet is like the artists of earlier religious societies, whom Gadamer says did what they did in order that their art might be accepted and take its place as part of their society's self-expression. The quotation from Richard Kearney also applies. If mimesis means bringing out hidden dimensions, that's what Eliot is getting at too with his insistence that one cannot substitute other words. The actual words, in their ordering, with their sounds, and with their resonances, work mimetically.[17] Though Eliot and the student are indeed discussing a bit of poetry, Ricoeur's broadened definition of "poetics" also applies.

In the paragraphs leading up to this illustration, Williams stresses the importance of the relationship between poetry and reality: "the poetic process is first a kind of apprehending of the environment that blurs conventional boundaries of perception—not to dissolve the actuality that is there but to bring out relations and dimensions that ordinary rational

---

16. Williams, *Grace and Necessity*, 30–31.

17. This is one reason why it is inadvisable to alter the syntax of poetry to fit your own if you are quoting poetry in an essay.

naming and analysing fail to represent."[18] Once again let's take the quotation a bit at a time.

As in other readings in these two chapters, the emphasis is twofold. There is a blurring of "conventional boundaries of perception." These "conventional boundaries" have to do with the patterns and expectations that we all put in place to help ourselves navigate our way through ordinary life, an ordinary day. Such boundaries are expressions of a certain understanding of rationality, yet they impede us from recognizing or appreciating something *more* in the reality we encounter.

The phrase "the actuality that is there" affirms art's contact with reality. Many people are so accustomed to thinking of art as "subjective" that it can be hard to take in the claim being made. Let me repeat it: poetry does not dissolve *the actuality that is there*. Rather, poetry helps to "bring out" relations and dimensions and enlarge one's sense of the actuality that is there.

The nod to metaphor is particularly noteworthy in this context. Williams tells us that metaphor is "inescapable." Its ubiquity, even when one is trying to be very disciplined in one's descriptions, attests a rich view of reality: "a sense of objects as it were carrying with them a charge of feeling that links them to other objects."[19] Metaphor makes sense in an environment best characterized as "belonging-to." Williams too stresses this way of conceiving reality. He writes, "It is all to do with things 'being more than they are.'"[20]

Williams also supplies a way of thinking about rationality and knowing that takes into account such an environment: "knowing is always a form of participation in the active intelligible life of an object, reproducing itself in the life of the subject."[21] Rationality has come under fire as being associated with ordinary ways of perceiving. Elsewhere, those "ordinary ways of perceiving" have been connected with being male, white, repressed. Rationality itself has come under extreme pressure; we have seen that it has even been treated with disdain. Here it is ultimately salvaged. Problems result from the modern conception of subjects and objects in isolation from one another, without awareness of an antecedent "belonging to an order of things," as Ricoeur put it. Words, in a participatory context, are neither concepts nor do they *represent* realities. Rather, they "'catch' and establish certain relations

18. Williams, *Grace and Necessity*, 28.
19. Williams, *Grace and Necessity*, 28.
20. Williams, *Grace and Necessity*, 29.
21. Williams, *Grace and Necessity*, 30.

or resonances."[22] That understanding informs Eliot's otherwise strange response to the inquisitive student.

Poetic Participation

Let's get back to reading some literature, for one does not want to suppose that participation can only be learned about by reading theory. If Eliot is right, then clearly poetry itself contributes to what comes to be called literary theory. With Ricoeur, one might say that theory, at least in some of its forms, belongs to "poetic discourse." Poetry and fiction propose themselves as trustworthy guides and themselves have things to say about the nature of reality and what it is to engage in interpretation. In this section, then, we are looking at poems that don't just *illustrate* what hermeneutics might be getting at. They themselves teach us what hermeneutics can mean.

The following poems and reflection all illumine participation-in or belonging-to a greater reality. Some accentuate the role of the "I"; all posit—through form as much as through content—a moreness: "hidden patterns and hitherto unexplored meanings." They propose simultaneously a wholeness or fullness from which the particular, the subject or the object, draws its being. Yet it's not as though the particular is simply part of a larger whole. Rather, the whole is revealed or shines through the particular. Paradoxically, the specificity and the uniqueness of the particular is preserved and deepened in the midst of its manifesting wholeness, unity, beauty, meaning. This phenomenon reinforces Macmurray's observation that, when we use our senses in a full way, "we come alive in them, as it were, and this opens up a whole new world of possibility."[23]

Hidden Presence

"The Hid, Here," by Canadian poet Margaret Avison, announces the possibility of revelation in its title. One immediately notices the strangeness of aspects of the description: "Big birds fly past the window / trailing strings . . ." (1–2); "Big trees become designs / of delicate floral tracery" (4–5). Some readers might not be shy of critiquing the awkwardness, even clumsiness, of the simile comparing the Milky Way to a football. Conventional

---

22. Williams, *Grace and Necessity*, 31.
23. Macmurray, *Reason and Emotion*, 22.

boundaries of perception begin to give way, the oddness of metaphoricity invites reflection on its inexhaustibility.

An awareness of otherness and transcendence accompanies this description. The poem evokes somewhere, something, beyond the Milky Way, which itself "lobs towards that still unreachable elsewhere" (9). The word "still" reminds us that the "elsewhere" confounds all our best efforts to grasp it and in some way reproaches them with its stillness. It hasn't gone anywhere—how is it that we haven't been able to find it? But wait. The sense of a fullness, of a Place, isn't elsewhere at all, or only so. It is "hid, here." It is hidden within the particular, a "bud," "nest-stuff," "bright air" (10). This is the longest line of the poem by far: the details of life are infinitely describable. In such a world, even the window, let alone the person looking out on the scene of everyday beauty, shares in what it reveals and waits expectantly. Nothing is truly inanimate. Windows were designed for such pleasures, crafted by glaziers who have dignity of their own and who infuse it in their work, no matter how mundane it may have become. Who knows if the football is genuinely leather and expertly sewn or a cheap plastic knock-off. It too, kicked expertly or thrown haplessly, participates in the drama of creation.

"Colours and Light"

George Herbert's poem "The Windows" (1633) likewise draws together the animate and the (apparently) inanimate. The windows in question are the stained glass of a church and the annealed lives of imperfect pastors expected to practice what they preach. The poet Herbert, himself a priest in the Church of England, would remind them, and himself, of this fact.

Yet how can preachers fully convey in their lives what they say from their pulpits? They preach "thy eternal word" (1), God's self-revelation in the Bible and in the Word made flesh, who is the second person of the Trinity. The poem takes on precisely the question of how particulars (in this case imperfect pastors) can contain and express the ineffable whole. The fact that the preacher is "a brittle, crazy glass" (2) only makes matters all the more unfathomable. The precise and inflexible /t/, the harshness and zaniness of "crazy," and the passivity of "glass" together assert the situation's intractability. Yet "Yet" (3) pulls the reader up short: the stanza affirms a vision of grace, of wholeness, and of healing.

In fact, the particular is the site of this mystery. Jesus is neither a principle nor some sort of universal good man. He has his own story, his own history; he is in history. He is also God. *That* gospel life anneals with the irreducibly specific lives of particular preachers, and those of others too. That's where the mystery lies, and that's where the strange vulnerability of truth can be discerned, for only faith can see the divine in human things. The world of the poem is imbued with this paradox.

Herbert plays with combinations of particularity and fullness. The pairings "Doctrine and life, colours and light . . ." (11) take the shape of a chiasm or X. "Doctrine" indicates a body of truths that are supposed to make a whole; a "life," meanwhile, is unique, personal, the place where "doctrine" is applied, however imperfectly and idiosyncratically. Unity precedes specificity. Then the pattern is reversed. "Colours" come from a specific life, with all its individual liveliness; they are manifold, multiple, separating into prismatic streams from a single, unified "light." If one were to construct a logical analogy, one might say:

> As doctrine is to life, so light is to colors.

The fact that Herbert subverts such a logical construction contributes to the mystery, the puzzle, of how universals and particulars go together. Make no mistake, though: for Herbert, they do! The "light" and "life" in this line, meanwhile, constitute an internal half-rhyme that itself combines the whole and the particular. Somehow the individual and a unified truth can come together "in one" (11). That "one" is itself ambiguous. Is it the arch-particular, a single one? Or is it the one that indicates ultimate unity and wholeness, as Plato would have it? The line ends at this point, drifting into space on the page to be suspended in this mystery.

When the reader returns to the next line, if the whole and the particular do "combine and mingle" appropriately, and the ordinary preacher lives a life in keeping with the doctrine he preaches, then that life will be a source of "awe." They mightn't, though. A preacher's words can remain "alone," in which case they will disappear. Ominously, they may take someone with them into non-being. Like the line ending in "one," that ending in "alone" leads off into space at its end. They give contrasting instances of the mystery of the relationship between being, its source, and nothingness. They also rhyme, bound together to form an even deeper mystery that enfolds them both.

"Bound with Love"

Dante (1265–1321) was the first major European poet to write in a vernacular language rather than in Latin. As such, he declared that local languages associated with specific places had value that could challenge the authority of the universal language of the church and of state administration. Did he no longer believe in the language of doctrine? Did he no longer believe in a unified truth? *The Divine Comedy*, a poem that took him over twenty years to compose, carries this question like a burden throughout its three parts. Ultimately, though, it attests a unified vision as well as loving attention to particular stories. Even the lives of the individuals he places in hell find meaning in a cosmos governed by God.

Dante meditates on this paradox in the one hundredth canto, the one that concludes the whole project. In this closing meditation, he plays with the same tension we see in Herbert between particulars and unities:

> O abbondante grazia ond' io presunsi
> > ficcar lo viso per la luce etterna,
> > tanto che la veduta vi consunsi!
>
> Nel suo profondo vidi che s'interna,
> > legato con amore in un volume,
> > ciò che per l'universo si squaderna;
>
> Sustanzia ed accidente, e lor costume,
> > quasi conflati insieme, per tal modo
> > che ciò ch' io dico è un semplice lume.
>
> La forma universal di questo nodo
> > credo ch' io vidi, perchè più di largo,
> > dicendo questo, mi sento ch' io godo.[24]

> O abundant grace, by which I presumed to pierce the eternal light with my gaze, so much so that I exhausted my sight there! In its depth I saw that it contained, bound with love in one volume, that which is truly scattered throughout the universe: substance and accident and their modes fused together, as it were, in such a fashion that that of which I speak is a simple light. The universal

---

24. Dante, *Paradiso*, 33.82–93.

form of this union I believe I saw, because in saying this I feel that I rejoice ever more.[25]

"Abundant grace" and "the eternal light" affirm an all-embracing unity; "I presumed," "my gaze," "I exhausted," "my sight" all insist on the poet's individual presence as a person. There is no absorption here, no loss of selfhood, even as the poet is caught up in ecstasy.

The "light" to which Dante has just referred is also a book, "bound with love." Like light, a single book symbolizes the unity of all things. The contents—or the leaves—of this book, however, are "scattered" throughout the universe. In the language of Dante's time, the very notions of unity (substance) and particularity (accident) are "fused together." In another paradox, the poet says he experiences a mystical vision of the "universal form," the hid, within "this union." The word translated as "union" is *nodo*, a medieval Italian word that denotes heterogeneity, hybridity, and multiplicity.

In the midst of this ecstatic experience, Dante reports that he tells of what he believes he saw and how he felt his joy expand. His experience involves rational reflection fused with faith. In telling of his experience in the way that he does, he gives it a specific form—it becomes a human work. At the same time, he has claimed its universal value, a mark of its greatness as a poem. The Italian word translated as "I believe," which has the connotation here of thinking as much as believing, is *credo*; it comes from the same Latin root that gives us the words "creed" and "credible." Dante affirms both the uniqueness of all that is and its having meaning as part of a unified whole. His is also an experience of joy. Properly appreciated, reason combines with emotion. In this context, joy is all-embracing and holistic, though, paradoxically, it begins as a specific experience and is capable of expanding infinitely. There is no question here of a rationality that tries to order, explain, and control all that is.

Mystery and Delight

One of Rowan Williams's great talents is an ability to say *a lot* in a little space. His short description (5:04 mins) as then-Archbishop of Canterbury of the royal wedding between Kate and William captures a great deal. He holds together the infinite depth of an individual reality and holistic

---

25. The translation is my own. My thanks to Roberta Cauchi-Santoro and Eric Wallace for their assistance. My thanks also to Lauren Byl for pointing me to Courtney Langdon's 1921 translation, which I found particularly resonant.

(social) meaning. For him too, both realities participate in the mystery of the divine life. A marriage, any marriage, reveals the individual, as well as social and divine reality. Williams gestures to the habits of a rationality that privileges *use*—from the clamorings of celebrity culture to the technicalities of presenting an event for global consumption. The Archbishop, however, manages to transform the pressures of the moment into a meditation of great simplicity and generosity. A gifted interpreter, Williams *reads* the *text* of this very public wedding.

He sounds the theme of participation straightaway with the notion of a person having endless depths: "There's always going to be more of you to discover";[26] "there's a mystery, a delight, at the heart of human beings."[27] Rather than have couples imagine a (potentially) dreary challenge to fulfil an obligation, Williams would reorient those contemplating the meaning of marriage in the direction of a richly rewarding and ongoing project of discovery. He invites people to develop a sense of the self as having infinite depths.

In connection with this view of commitment to a spouse, friends and family figure prominently. One might say that a wedding has the capacity to reveal an enlarged meaning of social relations. Williams hints that marriage indicates that we could always see that we are beings who belong to one another and to a reality beyond ourselves. A wedding merely accentuates the reality to which our senses are dulled. To be a participatory being means more, of course, than that we do things with others. It means that we discover more of who we are in all kinds of relationship. Williams presses this point. In the case of a very public wedding like William and Kate's, the involvement of so many people gives us something like a picture of being—*everything* connected, resonating. Of course, such resonance has to do with a "mystery" beyond the technology of television and social media. Ultimately participation happens before God and, for Williams, in God. Marriage as vows made before God and as conducted in the sight of God is a sign of reality's participation *in* God.

The witnessing of onlookers at any wedding is to be thought of as much more active than mere curious amusement or distraction. Williams charges all of us with a responsibility to activate and make more consciously real what is true on some level already: that we depend on one another and have an active part to play in one another's lives. He then

---

26. Williams, "Royal Wedding," 0:41.
27. Williams, "Royal Wedding," 0:53.

returns this understanding to the level of each unique person. Bearing witness to the promises and commitments of others can inspire us to find depths of commitment within ourselves.

It's already a small advance to recognize that one can analyze a YouTube video as a cultural text. But that's not at all the only text in view here. A wedding ceremony is itself also a text capable of being read. In the nature of things, it necessarily *will* be read one way or another, for we are interpretive beings and we read a great many "texts" each and every day.

Conclusion

William Carlos Williams's story "The Use of Force" might make one skeptical about what one is looking at in the scene depicted in Norman Rockwell's *Doctor and Doll*. Yet images of rationality in that picture find themselves caught up in something more. The diploma, the books, the doctor's gray hair, the stethoscope, the black attire all indicate the sitting figure's credentials. It's easy to sentimentalize what's going on. The doctor indulges the little girl, he enters into play with her, he takes her seriously. The stakes are high for her. She is at least as worried about being taken seriously as she is about her doll's health. She has made herself vulnerable to him, trusting him to make the effort and have the skill to enter into the world of her imagination properly. She has exposed her doll's heart; she has also exposed her own.

Rockwell confronts us with a similar choice as well. If we are content to sentimentalize the scene we will fail to appreciate the delicate demands of play. We will also fail to recognize that our own position resembles the doctor's. Not only does Rockwell invite us to imagine ourselves entering into the world of a child, he also challenges us to look with him as an artist, to enter into his imaginative openness to the world. If we might treat the child condescendingly, the artist is less easily disposed of, though many people treat artists as they do children.

The doctor looks up and away in a vacant stare of extreme concentration, though it may here be only feigned. Whatever his disposition, the red of the picture likewise channels the viewer's gaze upward and to the left in a U-shape that courses through the figures. It runs from the scrolling of the diploma down through the spine of the leaning book, the girl's beret, her scarf and skirt, then up through her mitten, which doubles as the doll's heart, the stethoscope, the good doctor's flushed face, and the leaning post and flag on the card tucked into the frame. The two candles on top of the desk, barely used, aren't needed in the cold light of day, but suggest that they might sometimes be lit in acknowledgement of a reality beyond the picture's border to which human aspirations, play, and achievements also gesture.

A participatory view of reality, like the other theories examined, challenges ordinary ways of perceiving. By implication, what one thinks of as rational also needs revising in its terms. Yet a participatory or hermeneutical view does not encourage the would-be theorist to disparage rationality or consign human meaning to the realms of arbitrariness and violence. Rather, the critique of rationality in literature and theory, in what Ricoeur calls "poetic discourse," can encourage a deeper commitment to rationality and to mystery at one and the same time.

Language and the Critique
of Rationality

9

Introduction to Section III

Language and the Rise of Theory

It is time to turn our attention to language. This may seem an odd thing to say in a book about literary theory. Isn't the study of *literature* automatically about language?

The study of language has its own history in philology and linguistics. It gets taken up in philosophy, especially in continental Europe, in a way different from the way it is treated as part of English as a discipline through most of the twentieth century. The English "department" at the University of Oxford includes "English Language" and "Literature" in its title. Once upon a time, J. R. R. Tolkien and C. S. Lewis worked strenuously to renew the vision of what their discipline could look like. Both had a passion for language (though Tolkien was the more ardent philologist). Yet both also saw scope for placing more emphasis on themes and ideas. Lewis helped Tolkien push a revised syllabus for his lecture course through the English Faculty Board in 1931.[1] From the direction of philosophy, however, language was to make a massive impact on the study of English as well as most other arts disciplines (and the social sciences too). Lewis and Tolkien would have welcomed some of these, others they would not have been altogether happy about.

The reader may recall that, in their introduction to feminism, Rivkin and Ryan at one point draw special attention to the role of language. They observe that "Feminist literary criticism moves with time from the criticism of writing by men and the exploration of writing by women *to a questioning*

---

1. Carpenter, *Tolkien*, 147–49. Many introductions to literary theory will begin with the ways of studying literature that take shape at this time. They are known as versions of "formalism," "practical criticism," and "new criticism."

of what it means at all to engage with or in language."[2] Similarly, in the history of psychoanalysis, Rivkin and Ryan stress that Freud's ideas get updated in linguistic terms: "In the 1950s and 1960s, Lacan developed a Structuralist theory of psychoanalysis based on the linguistic theory of Saussure."[3] Similarly, the terms "heterogeneity, hybridity, multiplicity," so important to critical race theory, have meaning in the context of philosophical developments that can be traced back to a particular understanding of language.

Thinking about language, then, is integral to thinking about what various theories are trying to get at. Over time, a set of ideas and a cluster of terms became integral to the discussion of why what passes as "rational" isn't necessarily so. One of the main convictions held by most theorists is that *language itself* is complicit in establishing what appears to be universal and normative, but is in fact bound up with interests (the interests of gender, race, class, and so on). For several influential thinkers, language doesn't even need an "interest" with which to be complicit. In and of itself, it proffers both the normative, and a dark underside to the normative. With reference to "English the language" and "English the cultural institution," Rivkin and Ryan write, "The cultural misconstrual of the local for the universal could only endure for so long."[4] Language itself becomes a place associated with violence and *the* place where the notion of essences and universals is most concentrated.

The aim of this final section is to give readers a sense of how the conversation develops and a firm grasp of the implications of ideas about language for thinking about rationality. Emphasis will be placed on the set of synonymous words encountered in the Lowe reading: heterogeneity, hybridity, multiplicity, particularity, specificity; emphasis will also be put on understanding the thrust of mainstream theory in marshalling these terms.

The first step will be to look at an early, scientific view of language that appears to be quite commonsensical: I will invoke timelines some more! That scientific view is unsatisfactory in just the same way that an unexamined understanding of rationality has proven to be contestable. Friedrich Nietzsche, himself a philologist, reveals some of the problems in an avant-garde philosophical style. His views, written down in the 1870s and '80s, provide the lens through which *A Course in General Linguistics* (1916) will come to be interpreted. That text, the collected notes from a course taught by Ferdinand de Saussure, introduced a new discipline Saussure called semiology and a new way of thinking about language that came to be called structuralism.

2. Rivkin and Ryan, *Literary Theory*, 769/897, emphasis mine.
3. Rivkin and Ryan, *Literary Theory*, 393/571.
4. Rivkin and Ryan, *Literary Theory*, 1071–72/1100.

The person most influential in combining Nietzsche's way of thinking with some of Saussure's key ideas was Jacques Derrida. He began writing in the 1960s. The importance of the 1960s for theory has already been seen in the history of the development of feminist and critical race theory. In this section, we will focus on that time period even more.

The development of the theory of psychoanalysis illustrates the importance of the turn to language for the development of literary and cultural theory. One can see in the work of one theorist in particular how Freud's terminology gets updated, *while the commitment to critiquing and redescribing rationality remains the same.* Jacques Lacan deepens Freud's insights into our inability to see ourselves and the problems associated with perceiving ourselves as wholes.

Finally, the implications of theory for the study of history will be considered. In a very important way, the study of history crystallizes the central issues raised in theory, not excepting the linguistic ones! Historical perspective persistently calls attention to difference. It would seem that the language of heterogeneity, hybridity, and multiplicity really does matter most—unless the whole can reach us in the particular. In that case, specifics retain their irreducible importance, but so too does the whole, the universal, and the true. If it cannot, then rationality is another word for the arbitrary exercise of power, and one can only hope that that power is exercised benevolently.

The Prevailing Scientific and Commonsense View of Language

The scientific outlook has developed over time in the West. Its growth coincides with increasing perplexity over the place of religion in society. Generally, Western civilized culture has come to accept the description of religion proffered by one philosopher as "man's self-incurred immaturity."[5] One might note the similarity between that formulation and Freud's notion of the development of humankind.[6] The ascendancy of science has included a distrust of rhetoric; a reaction against this suspicion partly informs philosophy's turn to language in the twentieth century.

The Royal Society for the study of science was founded in England in 1660. It took as its motto, "Trust no man's word." In writing the early history

---

5. Kant, "What Is 'Enlightenment'?" np.
6. See Chapter 4 above, esp. 54–55.

of this society in 1667, Thomas Sprat described its members' attitude towards language. He wrote of rhetoric that its ornaments

> are in open defiance against Reason; professing, not to hold much correspondence with that; but with its Slaves, the Passions: they give the mind a motion too changeable, and bewitching, to consist with right practice. Who can behold, without Indignation, how many mists and uncertainties, these specious Tropes and Figures have brought on our Knowledge.

The founders of the Royal Society, in contrast, he assures us,

> have exacted from all their members, a close, naked, natural way of speaking; positive expressions, clear senses; a native easiness: bringing all things as near the Mathematical plainness, as they can: and preferring the language of Artisans, Countrymen, and Merchants, before that, of Wits, or Scholars.[7]

Tropes and figures, or metaphors, cause "mists and uncertainties" while, apparently, language can be brought near an ideal of "mathematical plainness."

One notices that Sprat draws a line between reason and the passions. Reason is very much in focus as that which needs to be defended. Hopefully, one can appreciate from the work of the previous chapters that what he means by reason already has a particular shape. Sprat's assumptions lead him to the conclusion he reaches in the second part of the quotation. (Ricoeur's distinction between types of referential function indicates one way, at least, in which those assumptions can be interrogated.)

Sprat may want to assure readers of scientist intentions, but he himself hasn't avoided metaphorical language. Careful readers have no difficulty spotting metaphors in Sprat's prose. Internally, "bringing all things near mathematical plainness" turns out to be a problematic goal. Theory helps to explain why. Yet the increasing pervasiveness of a scientific construal of reality has encouraged just this understanding of language. For many, it is to be thought of only as a symbol or a tool. Surely one can reasonably expect a one-to-one correspondence between word and thing. Difficult though it may be to attain, one ought to strive for mathematical plainness. Language is surely capable of delivering on such a promise. It may not, strictly speaking, be made up of numbers, but as a system of symbols, language can be made to serve ends similar to those of science as a tool for clear communication. What could go wrong?

7. Sprat, *History of the Royal Society*, 2.20.

10

Rationality Is Logocentric

Introduction

This chapter links three writers, Friedrich Nietzsche, Ferdinand de Saussure, and Jacques Derrida, and three stages in the development of modern literary theory. The title privileges a term used by Derrida to describe the negative tendencies of rationality. Nonetheless, all three emphasize the notion of the "word" (Greek: *logos*) and its relationship with rationality. To link all three is to see at a glance the development of theory in linguistic terms.

One might revisit our timeline with the focus now on the nineteenth and twentieth centuries and previous developments as context.

| The Scientific Revolution and the Enlightenment | Friedrich Nietzsche (writing in the 1870s and 1880s) | Saussure's *Course in General Linguistics* (1916) | Jacques Derrida (begins writing in the 1960s) |

What we saw Eagleton refer to as "the modern age" is now in full swing, having begun in earnest with the scientific revolution and featuring increased confidence in detached rationality. Sometimes this "modern age," which stretches into the twentieth century, is called modernity. Sometimes, when one wishes to emphasize philosophical and cultural trends, especially that confidence in rationality alone, one will refer to the Enlightenment or to "the project of the Enlightenment." That project continues into the twentieth century as part of modernity, but with writers like Nietzsche it is already being called into question in the nineteenth. In fact, the Enlightenment project has its critics from its inception.

A Philosophical Source of Post-Structuralism

Friedrich Nietzsche (1844–1900) plays a crucial role in the development of literary and cultural theory. He offers a clear and mocking description of the outcome of the project of replacing religious belief with trust in human potentialities and, especially, in reason alone.

Belief—in the West that meant primarily Christian belief—had become increasingly problematic and unfashionable for a variety of reasons. One was that the early modern period brought with it a crisis of authority: who had it and why? This situation led Descartes to try to put the question of authority on a different footing, that of reason understood in a particular way, that is, separated from traditional structures of religious belief. Reason, he argued, began with *cogito, ergo sum* (I think, therefore I am). He had reached, he supposed, "first philosophy," as we have seen. Together with thinkers like Galileo and Francis Bacon, he inspired a confidence that increasingly took the shape of scientific detachment and mathematical description.

By the nineteenth century this confidence had come to take the form of positivism. It is another important term associated with a commitment to rationality alone: "Positivism had so dominated the early nineteenth century that few questioned the ability of the mind to achieve a purely factual, scientific knowledge of the world."[1] Nietzsche questioned this *scientific* certainty and arrogance. He saw that confidence in science as a foundation was philosophically untenable. He was concerned about commitments that passed themselves off as objective and disinterested. Nietzsche saw clearly that the notion of truth was at stake in the privileging of enlightenment as disembodied rationality: it could produce only a simulacrum of truth. To be told, as we sometimes are, that we live in a "post-truth" era, is to learn that we live in an era Nietzsche foresaw. In some ways he welcomed it. Some principled nihilists (and a great many people who have simply wanted to be philosophically fashionable) have, following Nietzsche, also declared themselves to be *against truth*. Such intellectuals have perhaps thought they could control the forms their Nietzschean principles could take. A glimpse at the German's essay "On Truth and Lying in an Extra-Moral Sense" shows something of what they have sought.

---

1. Rivkin and Ryan, *Literary Theory* 2, 262.

RATIONALITY IS LOGOCENTRIC

In this essay, Nietzsche claims that the power of the intellect is chiefly that of "dissimulation."[2] The intellect has the ability to hide the reality of things from us through the process of abstraction. In the paragraphs that follow this claim, Nietzsche focuses on the problem of rationality. The main theme of this book is at hand: "Now as a *'rational'* being he submits his actions to the sway of abstractions."[3] The notion of dissimulation accords well with the critique of rationality that is observable in modern theorists. This is one of their most important sources. To redescribe rationality, to say that it is male or white or repression, is to say that "rationality" as a seemingly pristine and obvious thing *is doing something* while no one is looking. This is what Nietzsche is drawing attention to in saying that its main power is dissimulation.

In developing this thought, Nietzsche puts two sets of terms in direct opposition to one another. He describes the change that an individual undergoes:

> he no longer suffers himself to be carried away by sudden impressions, by sensations, he first generalizes all these impressions into paler, cooler ideas.[4]

The word "generalizes" and the phrase "paler, cooler ideas" convey the problem associated with rationality. What is lost is that which is more embodied, visceral, and specific: "sudden impressions," "sensations." The next sentence sets up the same opposition:

> Everything which makes man stand out in bold relief against the animal depends on this faculty of volatilizing the concrete metaphors into a schema, and therefore resolving a perception into an idea.[5]

"The animal," "concrete metaphors," and "a perception" give way to "a schema" and "an idea."

I have jumped ahead in the essay to point out and follow the ribbon of the attack on rationality. Yet it is also present in his colorful earlier imagery. "Dissimulation" consists in our having reality hidden from us. He really means what he says when he writes, "Oh! That [man] could

---

2. Nietzsche, "Truth and Lying," 262.
3. Nietzsche, "Truth and Lying," 263.
4. Nietzsche, "Truth and Lying," 263.
5. Nietzsche, "Truth and Lying," 263.

but once see himself complete."[6] The lack of completeness is owing to abstraction. If it were possible, one would be aware of her or his *body*, its "convolutions," "blood-currents," and "vibrations."[7] Convolutions don't conform to a "schema" very easily. In this essay, "Nature" is not simply synonymous with the body or the animal, because even "Nature" is a concept that hides from man the proper knowledge of himself: "Nature threw away the key."[8] If we could see ourselves and if we had the courage to do so we would see that man "is resting on the pitiless, the greedy, the insatiable, the murderous . . . ."[9] In this dark emphasis, Nietzsche's thought anticipates that of Freud, who will be writing in a similar vein just a few decades later. Nietzsche has contempt for abstraction and for the scientific humanism that accompanies it.

A second noteworthy aspect of this essay is the way that Nietzsche links his assault on rationality with an attack on language. Establishing this connection is the main point of this section of this book: in literary theory, the attack on reason is conducted in linguistic terms.

Nietzsche doesn't mind metaphors. In fact, he loves them, as when he talks about "concrete metaphors." What he doesn't like is the way that our words for things only capture *part* of the reality of the thing: "We speak of a 'serpent'; the designation fits nothing but the sinuosity."[10] We do not capture the *whole* of something with our nomenclature. A related and greater problem is that our words for things do not convey the utter *singularity* and *uniqueness* of each individual reality, what it is as a whole in and of itself, be it a thing or an event.

His example of a leaf is justly famous:

> Every idea originates through equating the unequal. As certainly as no one leaf is exactly similar to any other, so certain is it that the idea "leaf" has been formed through an arbitrary omission of these individual differences, through a forgetting of the differentiating qualities, and this idea now awakens the notion that in nature there is, besides the leaves, a something called "the leaf," perhaps a primal form . . . .[11]

6. Nietzsche, "Truth and Lying," 262.
7. Nietzsche, "Truth and Lying," 262.
8. Nietzsche, "Truth and Lying," 262.
9. Nietzsche, "Truth and Lying," 262.
10. Nietzsche, "Truth and Lying," 263.
11. Nietzsche, "Truth and Lying," 263.

The word "leaf" applies to more than just the leaf in your hand as you admire its beauty, complexity, texture, greenness, translucency, and so on. No, the word "leaf" is already a generalization. It can't do justice to the particularity of *this* leaf. In fact, *any* word does *violence* to the particularity of each and every thing and experience. Language is inherently violent. Our way of using language is in cahoots with that rationalizing and abstracting and generalizing tendency that takes us *away* from "sudden impressions," "sensations," "the animal," "concrete metaphors," "a perception."

To feel Nietzsche's anguish is to appreciate a question that he bequeaths to subsequent philosophy, art, and culture. It is a challenge that he puts to scientists, as well as to anyone who uses language. It is one a person will want to feel acutely, with which one will want to sit, as Derrida did. At least until someone texts us ;)

In all seriousness though, Nietzsche jauntily raises a very difficult issue, and in the celebration of individual things gives us a glimpse of something very desirable.

Saussure and Structuralism

Ferdinand de Saussure's *Course in General Linguistics* and structuralism massively influence the development of theory. Though the *Course in General Linguistics* was published in 1916, its impact wasn't felt in literary studies for some time. It will be helpful to develop our timeline for the twentieth century further to understand how this influence unfolded. Russian formalists, British practical critics, and American new critics would establish the dominant expectations for how to practice literary criticism from the time that Tolkien and Lewis were updating methods in the English Faculty at the University of Oxford in the 1930s right through until the 1960s. These interpretive strategies were still firmly in place even after Saussure's ideas had begun to influence people in other disciplines, like the anthropologist Claude Lévi-Strauss. (He was active in the 1950s and 1960s and beyond.)

Saussure, *Course in General Linguistics* (1916) → Russian Formalism (1920s), New Criticism, and Practical Criticism (30s, 40s, and beyond) → Structuralism in other disciplines, eg Anthropology (1950s) → Saussure's influence spreads in Europe, especially in France (1960s) → Saussure and theory make a big impact in North America and England (1970s and 80s and beyond)

As we will see, the story of Saussure's influence, as far as literary theory is concerned, really takes off in the late 1960s (in France) and in the '70s and '80s in a wide swath of universities in North America and the UK.

For Saussure, language is a system with an underlying structure. Underneath a heterogeneity of speech utterances, one can find a pattern and structure. In their introduction to his work, Rivkin and Ryan stress his notion of order, referring to "rules of the system that lend order"; "an implied order"; "the internal system or order."[12] This order applies to other systems besides language: "Lévi-Strauss began to see that culture, like language, is a system characterized by an internal order . . . ."[13] The insight that such a structure could be found not only in language but in culture as a whole: *that* was the ticket to structuralism's future, at least in literary and cultural theory. Saussure's broad applicability led eventually to the transformation of "English" departments into departments of "English and Cultural Studies" or departments of "English and Film Studies" and so on.

In encountering Saussure, and to do justice to the way Rivkin and Ryan introduce his text, the would-be theorist wants to capture a second main point as well. In the first place, Saussure emphasizes an underlying structure to language as a whole; in the second he draws attention to the nature of the linguistic sign. Saussure gives the term "sign" specific meaning that we can readily grasp. In broad terms, he applies the same structural logic on the level of the sign that he does to language as a whole. Saussure's ideas will lead him to subvert the naïve view of the correspondence between word and thing that Thomas Sprat articulated in the seventeenth century. These ideas too have implications that will be very far-reaching.

12. Rivkin and Ryan, *Literary Theory*, 53/131.
13. Rivkin and Ryan, *Literary Theory*, 53/131.

Literary and cultural theory rejects scientific abstraction and rigidity, but the story is more complicated than that. One might expect that Saussure, over and over again given pride of place in the story of theory's advent, would subvert modernity's love affair with science. Yet that is not the case. The editors use language with thoroughly scientific connotations to describe what Saussure thinks about language and how to approach it: "frozen in time"; "cut transversely"; "the scientific impulse"; "skeleton"; "genetic code"; "tokens."[14] For Saussure, language differs from individual acts of speaking, and he emphasizes this point in terminology redolent of detached observation: "Language is a well-defined *object*"; "language, unlike speaking, is something that we can study separately"; "indeed, the science of language is possible only if the other elements are excluded."[15]

So Saussure challenges the view of language and words that was typical of scientists in the seventeenth century. Yet one does not want to project onto Saussure a notion that he is subverting science or seriously undermining confidence in Western rationality. For that, Derrida would need to make his vital contribution. Nonetheless, Saussure plays an important role, especially in the focus he puts on the idea of the sign and the terminology he introduces in connection with it.

Saussure on the Sign, Arbitrariness, and Difference

Saussure's conception of the linguistic sign proves to be very potent for undermining conventional notions of rationality, including scientific ones. It's the notion of the sign that carries the day, even though it's the notion of the structure that gives structuralism its name (!) and its broad appeal. We can soon see why. The notions of arbitrariness and of relative value have a central role to play.

What is a sign? When Saussure says, "Some people regard language, when reduced to its elements, as a naming-process only—a list of words, each corresponding to the thing that it names,"[16] the reader can take heart that they now have some familiarity with this sentiment in historical context. This is the view articulated by Sprat in the seventeenth century.

14. Rivkin and Ryan, *Literary Theory*, 53/131.

15. Saussure, *Course in General Linguistics*, 59, emphasis mine. (This section was not included in the third edition of Rivkin and Ryan's anthology.)

16. Saussure, *Course in General Linguistics*, 61/138.

It repays to labor with Saussure over what he does next. His first claim about the word as a linguistic unit is that it is "a double entity, one formed by the associating of two terms."[17] Let's not overlook the fact that this sort of statement posits and describes a structure: Saussure's conception of the sign contributes to his structuralism. More importantly, Saussure is very clear that the "two terms" are *not* "a thing and a name."[18] Rather, both terms refer to aspects of a psychological entity, the linguistic unit as belonging entirely in the head.

With this unit, Saussure nonetheless makes a distinction between the "concept" and the "sound-image" that is important to catch. The "sound-image" is "the psychological imprint of the sound."[19] It is "sensory" or *more* material than the concept, "which is generally more abstract."[20] Saussure substitutes the word "signifier" for "sound-image" and "signified" for concept. WARNING! If one thinks that the word "signified" refers to the thing in the world, one has reverted to the basic pre-Saussurean idea of "thing" and "name" (signifier being the name). One will run into confusion and frustration later. That thing in the world can be called the *referent*. It's not the signified; the signified is the *concept*-half of the double-sided *psychological* entity.

This distinction concerns Barbara Johnson in a piece called "Writing." Johnson is mindful of how Saussure's interests might appear to distance him from those of contemporary theory, not only with his emphasis on an underlying order but in the very way he talks about the sign. He seems to be overwhelmingly interested in concepts and scientific-sounding structures. Johnson makes an important clarification of how this theory of the sign came to be applied:

> Saussure's suspension of interest in history and the external world would seem to place him at the farthest remove from Marxism. But theorists of writing saw a connection between the signifier/signified relation and the materialism/idealism relation: If the signifier was the material condition of the existence of ideas, then the privileging of the signified resembled the fetishization of commodities

---

17. Saussure, *Course in General Linguistics*, 61/138.
18. Saussure, *Course in General Linguistics*, 61/138.
19. Saussure, *Course in General Linguistics*, 61/138.
20. Saussure, *Course in General Linguistics*, 61/138.

resulting from bourgeois idealism's blindness to labor and to the material conditions of economic existence.[21]

The first part of this quotation establishes the apparent unlikeliness. Saussure seems to distance himself from the world of particulars and sensory experience, a world that is of special concern to Marx. Yet Johnson draws out how the language of signs gets applied. In the phrase "connection between the signifier/signified relation and the materialism/idealism relation," the signified is on the same side of the divide as idealism; as Saussure's *concept*, the signified is the equivalent of the idealizing or the fetishizing of the produced commodity. The signifier, meanwhile, is on the same side as *materialism*. This equivalence will be totally missed if one thinks of the "signifier" as the word and the "signified" as the thing. The signifier is associated with the *more material* sound-image, the signified with the less material *concept*. The *signifier* comes to be associated with the reality of the labor and material conditions that the bourgeois ignore. As the signifier is to the signified, so labor is to the commodity. If, say, buying a cup of coffee makes one think only of the coffee itself, how warm it will feel in one's hands, how delicious it will smell, how great it will taste, well, what's happening is that the consumer is fetishizing and idealizing the commodity. Advertising encourages such activities. What is being forgotten, meanwhile, is the way that cup of coffee reached the consumer and how little others at the source may have been paid in order for you to get your relatively inexpensive cup of coffee *and* for the company to make its significant profit at the same time.

Another important implication of recognizing that both signifier and signified belong to a *psychological* entity is that Saussure is entrenching earlier developments. Following Descartes, Saussure privileges the *thinking self*. He locates meaning in the subject, that is, in the mind of the person doing the perceiving. In his context, this emphasis destabilizes the notion of rationality as detached and objectivizing, but it perpetuates a construal in terms of subjects opposed to objects. In other words, Saussure's ideas may bring changes to the ways people think about language, but premodern ideas about participation remain distant.

In Saussure's *Course in General Linguistics,* one can observe that two main points arise out of the discussion of the two-sided sign. The first is the arbitrariness of the connection between the two sides: "The bond between the signifier and the signified is arbitrary."[22] Arbitrariness means, primarily,

21. Johnson, "Writing," 342/530.
22. Saussure, *Course in General Linguistics,* 62/139.

that the signifier "actually has no natural connection with the signified."[23] This amounts to a strong declaration that language does not belong to the being of things. This emphasis lies at the heart of a distinction between the theories studied in the first section of the book and those considered in the second. In the second, one will recall, one kind of referentiality is obliterated *in order to make evident another*. For all the commentators in the second part, there is some sort of connection between word and thing, a resonance, a "belonging-to," a "participation in." For Saussure, language only works in a symbolic way, like mathematical symbols. Sprat's way of thinking about language is mathematical, not participatory. The emphasis on arbitrariness in Saussure, however, puts pressure on the earlier view of correspondences between words and things as imagined by Sprat.

Saussure takes pains to emphasize the point that arbitrariness does not leave the individual speaker in charge of signification. Some people no doubt jump too quickly from arbitrariness to the idea that Saussure underwrites extreme individual freedom. He does not. Nonetheless, the insistence on the separation of language from the being of things reinforces the stress on human volition. His view of language privileges human manipulation and control.

Saussure's second main point about the nature of signs is as important as the first one, if not more so. The heading "The Linear Nature of the Sign" merely introduces the feature within linearity that more properly fascinates the Swiss linguist. For him, the *interdependence* of terms is very significant. Signs are meaningless on their own; they find their meaning together with other signs: "Language is a system of interdependent terms in which the value of each term results solely from the simultaneous presence of the others."[24]

This observation reinforces a very important feature of Saussure's view of language, namely his distinction between values and signification. In Saussure's view, values and language have no natural or innate relationship with one another. The full significance of the linearity of the sign system comes through in subsequent sections: "The conceptual side of value is made up solely of relations and differences . . .";[25] "Signs function, then, not through their intrinsic value but through their relative position";[26] the

23. Saussure, *Course in General Linguistics*, 62/140.
24. Saussure, *Course in General Linguistics*, 66/169.
25. Saussure, *Course in General Linguistics*, 68/171.
26. Saussure, *Course in General Linguistics*, 68/171.

signifier is "constituted not by its material substance but by the differences that separate its sound-image from all others";[27] and, "in language, there are only differences *without positive terms.*"[28] As one small example, the difference between "mop" and "top" produces two different, meaningful words. All of these phrases underscore the importance of an environment in which differences can be discerned.

Saussure's insights into arbitrariness and linearity elevate the role of human communities, if not of individual speakers, in what language means and how it comes to function in theory. His analysis of linguistics gives rise to a large vocabulary of technical terms. It also encourages a structural way of thinking both about language and culture. In the foregoing discussion, we have only just begun to sensitize ourselves to the triad of technical terms sign-signifier-signified. Much more could be said. Yet, thinking of the forest-and-trees analogy, I would have readers recognize the importance of arbitrariness and difference in Saussure's description of language. I would further have one appreciate how Saussure's view upsets a commonplace assumption about correspondences, one at work in Sprat, for example. Thirdly, though, I would have one suspend belief that the change in views involves an either-or. Both Sprat's and Saussure's views emanate from a scientific construal of reality.

Derridean Deconstruction

To turn to Derridean deconstruction at this point might seem like a very short step to take. After all, when one starts reading about Derrida, the term "difference"—so important to how Saussure thinks about the linear relationship of signs to one another—crops up all the time. Furthermore, the Frenchman approvingly quotes Saussure: "Saussure had only to remind us that the play of difference was the functional condition, the condition of possibility, for every sign";[29] "it was Saussure who first of all set forth the *arbitrariness of signs* and the *differential character* of signs . . . ."[30] Yes. Let's notice the positive influence of Saussure more than fifty years on.

Yet, in their introduction to Derrida, Rivkin and Ryan strongly emphasize the difference (sorry, I couldn't resist) between him and Saussure.

27. Saussure, *Course in General Linguistics*, 69/171.
28. Saussure, *Course in General Linguistics*, 70/172, emphasis his.
29. Derrida, "Différance," 281/477.
30. Derrida, "Différance," 285/481, emphasis his.

For them, the name Jacques Derrida heads a list of people whose thinking "is usually referred to as Post-structuralism because it departed so radically from the core assumptions of Structuralism."[31] A couple of paragraphs later, they return to the point: "What did Derrida do that was so revolutionary?"[32]

Let's hold off answering that for a moment or two. For now, one can at least take note of the term "post-structuralism," which is obviously meaningful relative to structuralism. Another word that is commonly associated with Derrida is "deconstruction." It too invites one to think about structures, at least as a point of reference. One might also note a third term in this context, postmodernism. I don't want to lunge toward a definition of this general term at this point, but it comes over the horizon with the others here. Deconstruction (or post-structuralism) is different from structuralism; but structuralism is still part of the shift towards theory and postmodernism.

To build up a textured understanding of structuralism and of reading practices between the times of Saussure and Derrida, one might look at readings that show what structuralism looks like in various disciplines, like folklore studies and anthropology. One might also examine the rehabilitation of the study of rhetoric in the twentieth century. That recovery goes hand-in-hand with the importance of Saussure. "One of the major intellectual revolutions of the twentieth century consisted of restoring importance to the study of language," Rivkin and Ryan report. "It began in linguistics and carried over into anthropology, philosophy, and the literary criticism of the Russian Formalists and the French Structuralists."[33]

Nonetheless, the main narrative thread running through the development of literary theory is the one that runs from structuralism to post-structuralism. In the second edition of *Literary Theory: An Anthology,* Rivkin and Ryan develop the story especially clearly. When it comes time to collect the readings that represent "Post-structuralism, Deconstruction, Post-modernism," they offer one generalizing paragraph. Then they devote the rest of the introduction to Derrida ("Introduction: Introductory Deconstruction").[34] No other introduction to a school of theory in their anthology focuses so resolutely on one figure. It is written with great clarity and loving attention.

---

31. Rivkin and Ryan, *Literary Theory* 2, 257.
32. Rivkin and Ryan, *Literary Theory* 2, 257.
33. Rivkin and Ryan, *Literary Theory* 2, 127.
34. Rivkin and Ryan, *Literary Theory* 2, 257–61.

If all contemporary theory hearkens back to Saussure, for these editors (and for many others) it also runs directly through Derrida.

It is time to return to the question of difference. If Saussure already stressed it, what makes Derrida "revolutionary"? One can grab the nettle in the following remark: "Yet, if all things are produced by difference, then the very criterion that separates signification in language from thought and reality . . . no longer holds."[35] For Saussure, language could only be studied on its own, a discrete object for scientific investigation. What made language a discrete object was that it could be distinguished from the world around it, from thought and reality.

So, while Derrida is indebted to Saussure and, like the Swiss linguist, relies heavily on the term "difference," he radicalizes structuralism. He gives shape to what comes to be called post-structuralism. The implications are dramatic. Rivkin and Ryan state them clearly: "That insight poses a threat to the metaphysical tradition in philosophy that Plato initiated."[36] This statement echoes something they had said earlier: "[Difference] recalled for [Derrida] the work of Greek philosophers who stood outside the dominant Greek tradition of Aristotle and Plato."[37] Derrida upsets the main tradition of metaphysics or philosophy in the West.

We need to revisit our timeline! The ideas to which Derrida appeals are sometimes called "pre-Socratic." One may recall that an earlier version of the timeline included both pre-Christian and Christian eras, but only mentioned Socrates, Plato, and Aristotle in the first. Now that pre-Christian part of the timeline needs to be extended a bit. One is focusing on the time of "ancient Greek philosophy," "classical Greek thought," or (more nebulously) "Greek conceptuality."

Pre-Socratic Greek philosophers (c. 1000–400 BCE)	Socrates (d. 399 BCE) Plato (c. 424–348 BCE) Aristotle (384–322 BCE)	Christianity AD (*anno Domini*)/CE

Aristotle had been Plato's student. Plato had written down his own ideas as well as those of his teacher Socrates. Socrates had famously been forced to drink hemlock as punishment for "corrupting the youth," getting them to think philosophically.

35. Rivkin and Ryan, *Literary Theory* 2, 259.
36. Rivkin and Ryan, *Literary Theory* 2, 259.
37. Rivkin and Ryan, *Literary Theory* 2, 258.

In Plato's writings, the beginnings of modern philosophy had indeed begun to be laid down. He made distinctions; he brought logic to bear; he fostered distance from the object of inquiry and initiated the tradition of the cool savant. If one sits down with a couple of volumes of Plato (chosen almost at random, if you like) and reads them for oneself, his delight in dialectical reasoning, of pitting one view against another, is readily apparent. (Anyone can do this; no one needs a special licence to read Plato and "get" him. He was a good teacher after all! Furthermore, like Socrates, he believed that philosophy, literally the love of wisdom, was possible for anyone.) Plato's way of doing philosophy highlighted the connection between thought and what the Greeks called *logos*. That word has come to mean "word." For the Greeks it included discourse, the reasoning process, and the notion of subject matter as well.

It's easy to exaggerate just how dialectical or logocentric Plato was. I want to take a moment to flesh out Plato's position a bit. Clearly, much is at stake. We need a narrative we can follow, but we can't be too hasty where Plato is concerned. One voice calling for hesitation belongs to a mid-twentieth-century existentialist. William Barrett cautions,

> Even in Plato, where the thought has already become more differentiated and specialized and where the main lines of philosophy as a theoretical discipline are being laid down, the *motive* of philosophy is very different from the cool pursuit of the savant engaged in research. Philosophy is for Plato a passionate way of life.... [38]

Barrett does not want his readers to equate classical Greek philosophy with the highly technical, detached, quasi-scientific practice it becomes in the modern world, particularly in universities in England and North America. The Canadian philosopher George Grant takes a similar tack. He critiques another famous account of Plato as inaugurating a long history of metaphysical error (Derrida's was not the first) by countering that Plato is motivated throughout by a love for justice.[39]

Derrida's critique of Plato leads him to look further back in time. He finds in pre-Socratic philosophers like Heraclitus, in contrast to Plato's desire to differentiate, "the blending together of things over their discreteness or separable identities."[40] Socrates and his students made distinctions; pre-Socratics held things together.

---

38. Barrett, *Irrational Man*, 5.
39. Grant, *English-Speaking Justice*, 42.
40. Rivkin and Ryan, *Literary Theory* 2, 257.

There is a difference between the pre-Socratics and Plato, to be sure. However, one must take care not to caricature what Socrates's and Plato's innovations represent, as Barrett warns us. Furthermore, one wants to be cautious about supposing one can step outside of the tradition Socrates inaugurated. The difficulty is like that encountered if one supposes that one can overcome unconscious bias. For his part, Derrida expresses a desire and an awareness of a tradition's limitation.

Derrida and the Tomb of Language

To read Derrida can be overwhelming. Some, though, take to him like a duck to water. At the very introductory level intended here, I will point out just a few aspects of his approach. These can be easily missed as one tries to get one's bearings or find bottom in any given reading. One might try to comprehend the forest as a whole and in the process fail to identify a tree or two. The temptation is great, because the claim for his influence is great, and his own critique is as well.

To read Derrida effectively is to read him poetically, to enjoy the experience and to go with the flow. Even if one does not follow all of his moves, one can appreciate the vistas that appear suddenly and the feats he accomplishes through his own imaginative interpretation of various texts and cultural artefacts. In a talk he gave in Paris that became the 1968 essay "Différance," Derrida introduces his unique way of thinking about the term "difference":

> The verb "to differ" [*différer*] seems to differ from itself. On the one hand, it indicates difference as distinction, inequality, or discernibility; on the other, it expresses the interposition of delay, the interval of a *spacing* and *temporalizing* that puts off until "later" what is presently denied, the possible that is presently impossible. Sometimes the *different* and sometimes the *deferred* correspond [in French] to the verb "to differ" . . . .
>
> In the one case "to differ" signifies nonidentity; in the other case it signifies the order of the *same*. Yet there must be a common, although entirely different [*différante*], root within the sphere that relates the two movements of differing to one another. We provisionally give the name *differance* to this *sameness* which is not *identical*: by the silent writing of its *a*, it has the desired advantage

of referring to differing, *both* as spacing/temporalizing and as the movement that structures every dissociation.[41]

Derrida demonstrates a fondness for paradox in describing a "sameness which is not identical," which readers can relish on their own. I want, more prosaically, to highlight his attentiveness to something small, in this case the letter "a." He refers to the oral context for his Parisian address when he says, "For I cannot even let you know, by my talk, now being spoken before the Société Française de Philosophie, which difference I am talking about at the very moment I speak of it."[42] The fun that he is having (in French) with manipulating "a" and "e" cannot be heard. The confusion goes to his claim that "difference" does not have a stable reference point in reality. He is about to make that argument: "since from this point of view the difference between the *e* and the *a* marked in 'difference' eludes vision and hearing . . . ."[43] That clause serves as a reference to basic philosophical categories that he is in the process of rendering problematic. Having drawn attention to speaking, Derrida expresses dissatisfaction with a too easy distinction between speech and writing: "This difference belongs neither to the voice nor to writing in the ordinary sense."[44] His further point is that the study of *writing* is just as important as the study of *speech*.

Derrida's presentation, then, is highly theatrical or performative. It's easy for the perplexed reader to miss this point. The Frenchman has fun taking the letter *a*, his innovation in the word *difference*, imagining it as a capital, and from there imagining a pyramid and a tomb! If one ignores the mystique around deconstruction and postmodernism, in this example one can see that Derrida is engaging in a *very* detailed close reading. In "play," he takes the reality in front of him (here the letter *a*) very seriously.

The American philosopher Richard Rorty once said insightfully, "Derrida throws himself into the arms of the texts he writes about. . . . There is a difference between 'play' in the approbative sense . . . and what the know-nothings mean by 'frivolity.'"[45] Eagleton similarly reminds readers that Derrida is among those theorists who engage in "scrupulously close reading."[46] Derrida is a playful, not a frivolous, thinker.

41. Derrida, "Différance," 279/475.
42. Derrida, "Différance," 281/477.
43. Derrida, "Différance," 281/477.
44. Derrida, "Différance," 281/478.
45. Rorty, "Remarks on Deconstruction and Pragmatism," 14.
46. Eagleton, *How to Read a Poem*, 2.

In playing with language, he shows that it has "play." That is, like a steering wheel or bike handlebar that's loose, the details of language aren't tight or reliable. Reality as encountered through language isn't as stable as we'd like to think it is; when we put pressure on our intellectual assumptions, they don't hold up. This second sort of play opens up an abyss. It would appear that there is no ultimate meaning to human activity: "[reality] is a tomb that cannot even be made to resonate."[47] In choosing to compare the first letter of the alphabet with a tomb, he attacks one dimension of the *logos*, rationality as it is understood from Plato onward, as the basis or center of philosophical thought. He attacks Western philosophy as logocentric. As a beginning, this is enough deconstruction to think about.

Except here's one other thing: "deconstruct" is an intransitive verb. That means it doesn't cross over to an object, like a transitive verb does. The verb "trembled" is intransitive. In the sentence "The earth trembled" the verb *cannot* cross over to an object. Critics and readers don't deconstruct arguments or poems or anything else. Demolition teams don't deconstruct buildings. Arguments and cultural artefacts deconstruct. That is, their internal logic, the sense that they are rational, has limitations, if not inbuilt flaws, if not a tomb at its heart. The astute reader, theorist, or cultural critic makes this reality manifest.

Conclusion

If one can say that rationality is male, is white, is repression, one can also say that it is logocentric. To say so is to confront any number of logical assumptions, including the self-assurance of identity. Most significantly of all, it is to confront Plato and the tradition of philosophical inquiry Socratic dialogue helped to birth.

47. Derrida, "Différance," 281/477.

11

Rationality Is Real

Introduction

Literary theory, like art itself, deeply questions rationality: its reach and what it is. This critique crystallizes around language. Ferdinand de Saussure, in his rather scientific analysis, proposes that arbitrariness and difference figure prominently in linguistic meaning. In the right hands, these terms become the means of dismantling confidence in rationality and increasing suspicion that what passes for rationality masks power and violence.

This critique, especially by Derrida (but with the considerable influence of Nietzsche) looks pretty comprehensive. Nietzsche said that we ride on the backs of tigers, while Derrida questions the whole of the Western philosophical tradition from Plato onward.

The immediate aim now is to consolidate an appreciation of the significance of Saussure and language for literary theory by returning to psychoanalysis. It illustrates the impact of linguistic terminology. In the movement from structuralism to post-structuralism, the emphasis was placed on what made Derridean deconstruction different from and more philosophically radical than Saussurean structuralism. By contrast, to put the two versions of psychoanalysis side-by-side is not to emphasize philosophical radicalization. It is rather to appreciate the redescription of Freud's ideas in Saussurean language and to observe the extension of the critique of the notion of a unified self. The main person who undertakes this work, Jacques Lacan, like Freud destabilizes confidence in rationality. He associates it with a projection he calls "the Real"; what he calls "a lack," meanwhile, characterizes our actual condition. Freud's successor is also a reader of literature. This chapter revisits a short story Lacan considered closely, Edgar Allen Poe's "The Purloined Letter." It is a natural fit. Poe himself interrogates the shortcomings of rationality as conceived by an extremely efficient and thorough police force.

Lacan, I'm Your Father

Sigmund Freud wrote his influential work *The Interpretation of Dreams* in 1900, well before the publication of Saussure's *General Course in Linguistics* in 1916. His ideas about the id, the ego, and the superego, about repression, neuroses, and fetishes, remained popular in their own right through the 1970s and '80s and have long since entered popular consciousness.

Jacques Lacan (1901–81) is a Freudian psychoanalyst who applies Saussurean descriptions to important Freudian categories like the unconscious. As Rivkin and Ryan tell us, "In the 1950s and 1960s, Lacan developed a Structuralist theory of psychoanalysis based on the linguistic theory of Saussure."[1] Let's not forget when structuralism began to influence other disciplines in earnest, in the 1950s and '60s. Lacan was working with Saussurean ideas independently of Derrida.

Saussure, *Course in General Linguistics* (1916) → Russian Formalism (1920s), New Criticism, and Practical Criticism (30s, 40s, and beyond) → Structuralism in other disciplines, eg Anthropology (1950s) → Saussure's influence spreading in Europe, especially in France (1960s) → Saussure (and theory) making a big impact in North America and England (1970s and 80s and beyond)

It is not as though theory goes through Derrida and only through him, even though deconstruction is undeniably central to post-structuralism. Lacan was working out his most influential ideas as early as 1949, if not earlier. He is writing at roughly the same time as the anthropologist Claude Lévi-Strauss.

Lacan wants to rescue psychoanalysis from those who concentrate on the ego to the exclusion of the seething undercurrents that make up the id. In faithful Freudian fashion, this Frenchman insists on the importance of the drives and the unconscious: "the ego is constructed through

---

1. Rivkin and Ryan, *Literary Theory*, 393/571.

imaginary percepts and narcissistic fantasies, and it remains blind to its determinations by the drives, the unconscious, and its placement and construction in/by language."[2] Everything before the last phrase in the foregoing quotation is standard Freudian material. Lacan likes Freud and is faithful to him. Both are especially attuned to the way other psychologists are deceived about the solidity of the ego.

It's the last phrase in the quotation that might throw one: the notion that the ego is "placed" and constructed *by language*. That last phrase indicates the importance of language in Lacan's rethinking of Freud's ideas. The next couple of sentences in Rivkin and Ryan's introduction reinforce the importance of language for Lacan: "*Before language* we have no sense of self"; "it is *language* that gives us identity."[3]

At this point, in a compact and very important paragraph, Rivkin and Ryan turn aside from the emphasis on language to introduce Lacan's theory of how our sense of a unified self develops in childhood. This theory is important to introduce because it reinforces psychoanalysis's basic claim that the self is *not* truly unified. Lacan's theory of childhood is his own, but it shares the same basic orientation as Freud's: towards a self that is not in rational control of itself.

The rest of that paragraph then drives home this insight with some important terms and phrases. The Real is introduced as a state of fantasy with three features: "an impossible wholeness of self"; complete satisfaction of desires; *and a connection between word and object* of the sort Sprat wanted. Instead, we deal with an "initial fissure," "separation," and "the initial experience of being ripped out of an original *imaginary* fulness of being" which we thought defined us in our early unity with our mother.[4] As Lacan writes in an essay on an early stage of childhood development, "the important point is that this form situates the agency of the ego, before its social determination, in a fictional direction, which will always remain irreducible for the individual alone . . . ."[5] Rivkin and Ryan also refer to Lacan's signature phrase "lack-of-being," or simply our "lack." Our fundamental reality is that "we are constitutively alienated" rather than having a whole or stable identity.[6]

2. Rivkin and Ryan, *Literary Theory*, 393/571.
3. Rivkin and Ryan, *Literary Theory*, 393/571, emphasis mine.
4. Rivkin and Ryan, *Literary Theory*, 393/571, emphasis mine.
5. Lacan, "The Mirror Stage," 619.
6. Rivkin and Ryan, *Literary Theory*, 393/571.

There is no question that Lacan's understanding further upsets a view of the self as contained. Lacan, like Freud, calls one's attention importantly to the notion of limits. Certainly many people cling to the idea of a stable ego. It gives them a sense of control in the world. Lacan's chief point, like Freud's, is that one does not have the control one thinks one does.

Lacan's Unconscious and Saussure's Signifying Chain

At this point, I want to shift attention to the essay by Barbara Johnson that was introduced in the last chapter. Johnson explains how theorists have interpreted the signifier and the signified in a way that relates the signifier to more material aspects of lived reality. Beyond that clarification, her essay allows one to consolidate the basic idea that, through Lacan, psychoanalysis shares in the influence of Saussurean thought and develops in a post-structuralist direction. Johnson also helps one to encounter at greater length and greater ease the relationship between language and the unconscious.

Lacan plays an important role in the way that the application of Saussure's ideas developed. As Johnson reports, Lacan deployed Saussure's theory of the sign to say that the unconscious, that realm that never clearly or entirely discloses itself, is structured like a language. Specifically, he used the notion of the chain of signifiers, to which we have already been introduced in the *Course in General Linguistics*. His brilliant move was to compare signifiers to those various manifestations of repression, including dreams, neuroses, and fetishes. The repression is visible or manifest, the reality being repressed is not. Repression indicates the reality of the unconscious, that realm of the drives, though we don't really know what's going on down there.

Saussure's idea that signs have meaning in relation to one another *and only in relation to one another* gave Lacan a way of talking about the meaningful bits of a dream. As Johnson explains, each "knot of associations"[7] in a dream needs to be considered on its own. It's not clear how the knots within a dream actually relate to one another. It's the psychoanalyst's job to "read" the dream properly. A dream is like a rebus. Its parts connect together weirdly. Below is a rebus of some of Shakespeare's plays.[8]

---

7. Johnson, "Writing," 342/530.
8. The answers appear at the end of the chapter.

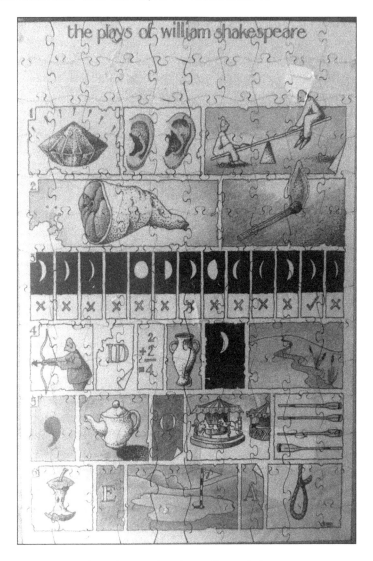

A rebus of some plays by William Shakespeare.

Johnson tells us that Lacan was one of the first thinkers to emphasize the signifier as the more material part of the sign.[9] With the signifiers in mind, he posited that knots of association in dreams act as a "signifying chain," though the signified is never revealed. This conceptualization allowed him to claim that the unconscious is structured like a language. Perhaps the

9. Johnson, "Writing," 342/530.

greatest single effect of this way of looking at things was the implicit suggestion that there is nothing at all of substance in the unconscious apart from this structure. It *generates* the "effect of signified," but there is no bottom, no substance at the core of the self, in fact no core at all. The notion that the unconscious is structured like a language made even more stark the Freudian claim that humans lack a solid ego.

One can see the effect of Lacan's Saussure-inspired claim very clearly in what happens to the notion of desire. In Freud's world, the unconscious realm is the home of desires that produce dreams, neuroses, and fetishes. In Lacan's world, desire is produced by an unconscious structured like a language. Desire does not indicate the existence of a core self, which Freud's account does, even if the latter is a debased version of Descartes's *cogito*. Quite the contrary. To see the difference between desire as producer and desire as product can feel like a bit of a mental trick. Perhaps it's not unlike the challenge of seeing the two different figures in each of the following two images.[10]

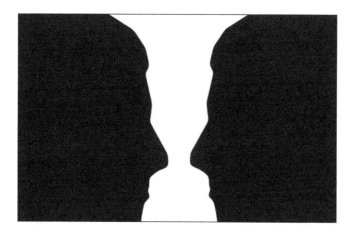

10. As with the Shakespeare rebus, the answers are given at the end of the chapter.

If it provides some small satisfaction to stare at these pictures until one sees both images in either of them, it also provides satisfaction to be able to see desire in the two different ways.

If, as Johnson has explained, the signified is an *idea,* to be able to focus on the signifier is a way to avoid being burdened by meaning and concepts. To focus on the signifier is to affirm material realities in and of themselves. Johnson refers to "what it might mean to *liberate* the signifier."[11] The vein of thought is similar to that of Nietzsche in his meditation on the leaf. He is seeking a way to delight in simply physical, bodily existence. An important aim in all of this is to achieve greater freedom. That freedom is associated with materiality itself and escape from the burden of meaning.

---

11. Johnson, "Writing," 345/530, emphasis mine.

Johnson provides a metaphysical context for the development of theory and its insistence on the pre-eminence of physicality:

> As early as 1953, in *Writing Degree Zero*, Roland Barthes [another leading theorist] had investigated the paradoxical relationship that existed in the nineteenth century in France between the development of a concept of Literature (with a capital L) and the growing sense of a breakdown in the representational capacities of language. Literature was in some ways being exalted as a substitute religion . . . .[12]

Johnson here makes a very important observation for any meaningful narrative about theory. Literary theory developed in a context in which religion had already been abandoned. The attempt was underway to put Literature in its place as a substitute. That's why the capital L is important.

Nietzsche had already anticipated and decried such substitutions. Johnson underscores theory's historical role. In an important sense, *theory blew the whistle on this project of investing Literature with a quasi-transcendent status*. This is by no means to say that theorists by and large wanted to turn back to religion. Not at all. What theory in its mainstream form wants is a more comprehensive and consistent recognition of the implications of the loss of religious belief or at least of a certain belief in representation. This desire for meaning, whether in humanism or science, is especially clear in Nietzsche. He does not limit his disdain to Christianity. He has contempt as well for the self-assurance of the sciences: in "Truth and Lying in an Extra-Moral Sense" they are squarely in his sights in his analysis of explanatory language. He also snorts in derision at what he knows the bourgeois will do with the death of God, namely exalt the human in place of the divine. In many ways, as Johnson realizes, mainstream theory offers a searching exploration of what is philosophically plausible once God and the substitutes for God have been discarded. Richard Rorty, cited in the last chapter, would include Derrida in such a project as well. He sees him as embodying

> the hope that human beings, once they have set God *and the various surrogates for God* to one side, may learn to rely on their own romantic imagination, and their own ability to cooperate with each other for the common good.[13]

---

12. Johnson, "Writing," 341/529.
13. Rorty, "Remarks on Deconstruction and Pragmatism," 14, emphasis mine.

Rorty too sees how the nineteenth century, in philosophy and literature alike, attempts to replace God with "surrogates." This is the context in which Johnson reviews the development of theory and establishes Lacan's importance.

Rationality as Procrustean Bed in "The Purloined Letter"

Lacan reads the story "The Purloined Letter." Why *this* story? A literary theorist can read *any* text through his or her preferred lens. For example, a competent feminist critic can find issues of feminist concern in *any* text. They can ultimately frame their approach to the text—whatever that text may be—as revealing a reality conceived in terms that concern the feminist. A critical race theorist can do the same—for *any* text; and so on for all literary theories. It is nonetheless noteworthy that Lacan chooses to (re-) read a story that already focuses on the issue of rationality. Theories align themselves especially well with particular stories or poems. The situation isn't quite so *entirely* random or arbitrary or "neutral" as it may seem.

Poe's story announces its interest in the question of what we mean by "rationality" even before it has begun. It opens with a quotation from Seneca, given in Latin. That quotation translates as the following: "There is nothing so odious to wisdom as excessive cleverness."[14] This statement in and of itself warns the reader to take care over the meaning of terms; it implies that wisdom and cleverness are not the same thing. This ambiguity urges the question, with which of the two is rationality to be more closely associated?

The story establishes an opposition between the way that Dupin conducts an inquiry and the way the Parisian police do (especially Monsieur G–, the prefect of the police). The opposition between them surfaces quickly when Dupin remarks, "'If it is any point requiring reflection . . . we shall examine it to better purpose in the dark.'" To this the prefect responds, "'That is another of your odd notions.'" Through Dupin, Poe introduces the paradoxical notion of seeing better in the dark, where seeing (or "reflection") means being able to understand the true nature of a problem. Poe implies that the data of day-to-day reality only serve to distract, and that real thinking involves the imagination, not merely processing the data of ordinary reality.

14. Poe, "The Purloined Letter," np.

At issue is the stealing of a compromising letter from the apartment of the royal woman to whom it was written. The police know who took the letter, "the Minister D–," and it is "'clearly inferred'" that he still possesses it. The trouble is that the police, despite having had the opportunity to search the minister's apartment often over an eighteen-month period of time, have not been able to recover the stolen document.

The police proceed through arduous effort, which has all the appearance of painstaking intellectual work: "'Why the fact is, we took our time, and we searched everywhere.'" Poe must have had fun writing this story and putting such lines in the mouth of a hapless functionary. Monsieur G– goes on for lines and lines describing the meticulous effort of his people:

> Why the fact is, we took our time, and we searched everywhere. I have had long experience in these affairs. I took the entire building, room by room; devoting the nights of a whole week to each. We examined, first, the furniture of each apartment. We opened every possible drawer; and I presume you know that, to a properly trained police agent, such a thing as a secret drawer is impossible. Any man is a dolt who permits a "secret" drawer to escape him in a search of this kind. The thing is so plain. There is a certain amount of bulk—of space—to be accounted for in every cabinet. Then we have accurate rules. The fiftieth part of a line could not escape us. After the cabinets we took the chairs. The cushions we probed with the fine long needles you have seen me employ. From the tables we removed the tops.

The effort at once underscores a commitment to rational endeavor even as it reinforces the obtuseness of the police and the futility of that trust. Poe suggests the paradox equally effectively in his writing style. The prefect speaks in clear, declarative sentences interspersed with furtive asides. The accumulation of short sentences gives his speech a breathless quality. The police cannot find the letter that is the object of desire.

Dupin, for his part, knows that he has to think like the person who hid the letter. He describes him as someone combining the qualities of the mathematician *and* the poet: "As poet and mathematician, he would reason well; as mere mathematician, he could not have reasoned at all . . . ." Genuine reasoning, for Poe, combines analytic or calculative capacity with artistic and creative prowess. Significantly, Poe does not dismiss reasoning, he affirms it: "he would reason well."

If genuine rationality combines these qualities, the failure to fuse them results not only in the absence of reason but something violent and deformed. Dupin says of Monsieur G–, "A certain set of highly ingenious resources are, with the Prefect, a sort of Procrustean bed, to which he forcibly adapts his designs." A Procrustean bed is an instrument of torture. A certain conception of rationality produces violence—"he forcibly adapts his designs"—and does not help one discover truth.

This is the environment in which Lacan elaborates his theory of the sliding chain of signifiers. "Our inquiry has led us to the point of recognizing that the repetition automatism finds its basis in what we have called the insistence of the signifying chain," he begins his seminar on the story.[15] That chain already challenges a certain conception of rationality, as has been discussed. For Lacan, the sliding chain of signifiers is uncoupled from signification. All that matters is the relationship between signifiers. The story takes shape in terms of the letter's position amongst the various agents, whom Lacan divides into three sets, within it: "We shall see that their displacement is determined by the place which a pure signifier—the purloined letter—comes to occupy in their trio."[16] In the story, the reader never discovers the content of the letter.

In this way, Lacan challenges any association between reason and discovery. That rationality could be satisfying in such a way—anyone's discovering the contents of the letter—is an illusion. Rationality may have such associations, but this conception is wrong. For a Lacanian psychoanalytic critic, rationality is itself an illusion. It works in tandem with the Real, the realm of wholeness, of unity, of attained meaning and knowledge. One never attains such wholeness or closure. Our more basic reality is one of perpetual lack. There is a fissure in our being that we perpetually try to overcome. The fact that we cannot do so dooms us to frustration as the playthings of a meaningless universe or sick god. We need psychic healing or maturation to appreciate our situation properly.

The Lacanian psychoanalyst is a real person, and her or his practice a real profession. Such psychoanalysts pursue the goal of reconciling the analysand (the person being analyzed) to their condition and to the nature of the universe. Therapy is an ongoing project. The illusions of the universe, which enter us from the days of our *very* early childhood, exert a perpetual and strong force.

15. Lacan, "Seminar on 'The Purloined Letter,'" np.
16. Lacan, "Seminar on 'The Purloined Letter,'" np.

Conclusion

In Lacanian psychoanalysis, we have a clear illustration of the influence of Saussure and the linguistic turn. Put side by side, Freudian and Lacanian psychoanalysis serve to illustrate in a very specific way the importance of the Swiss linguist. The category of "reason" or "rationality," so important to Freud, remains in focus; the terminology used to unpack its limitations now comes from the field that Saussure invented. That language and the way of thinking that informs it aid Lacan not only to interpret Poe in a new way, they allow him to explore the implications of Freud's notion of the unconscious in ways that his master never dreamed of. Desire becomes something even more elusive, though arguably even more indicative of the nature and perils of the human condition, at least from a psychoanalytical perspective.[17]

---

17. The plays in the Shakespeare rebus from the top are: *Julius Caesar*; *Hamlet*; *Twelfth Night*; *A Midsummer Night's Dream*; *A Comedy of Errors*; *Coriolanus*.

The first image can be seen either as a chalice or as two people in conversation with one another. The second image can (much harder, in my humble opinion) be seen either as a young woman looking away over her right shoulder, or as an old woman with a pronounced nose and protruding chin looking downward.

12

Rationality Is Unities

Introduction

There are a great many forms of literary theory, but in the 1990s one approach emerged as an umbrella for virtually all of them. Under it, many of the others could be applied to different texts and could often be combined. At the same time, this governing practice remained a recognizable form of theory in its own right. This theory was called new historicism.

New historicism is another title strongly associated with the notion that rationality is limited. Specifically, the word "historicism" implies particulars. As has been seen, rationality is, for theory, generally a negative term. It masks the real situation, in which appeals to neutrality hide the interests of specific groups or proclivities—rationality is male, rationality is repression, and so on. For the new historicist, rationality is unities. Unities obscure particularities.

Looked at in terms of unities, new historicism stands very close to Lacanian psychoanalysis. We have seen that the latter school itself decries unities, which it dismisses as so many attempts to gain access to the Real. New historicism stands close to other theories as well, such as critical race theory. Lisa Lowe emphasized heterogeneity, hybridity, and multiplicity. These are near synonyms for particularities. So too is the term "difference." Since most theories emphasize specificity, particularization, and the way "the dominant passes itself off as the universal" (to requote Rivkin and Ryan), historicism is a term that encompasses the denial of the universal as stressed by feminists, critical race theorists, deconstructionists, eco-critics, Marxists, disability studies theorists, trans-humanists, post-humanists, and others. As Rivkin and Ryan aver, "Literary study today is pervasively historical."[1]

---

1. Rivkin and Ryan, *Literary Theory*, 505/714.

Technically, the word "historicism" itself flags an overriding concern for the particular. So what's with the "new"? The situation with historicism is similar to that with psychoanalysis: the "new" comes after the turn to structuralism and to language with Saussure, and "new historicism" then takes off with the help of deconstruction. It aggressively reveals the philosophical implications of a strict allegiance to history. As with deconstruction, much of its impetus derives from Nietzsche.

In this chapter, new historicism is introduced in conjunction with ideas from Michel Foucault. With influential writings dating from the early 1960s onward, this figure serves as another reminder of the importance of that time period for the development of theory. As we will see, a standard anthology for the introductory study of literature, *The Norton Introduction to Literature,* gives evidence of the impact of this theory on traditional approaches. Meanwhile, F. Scott Fitzgerald's sobering story about the past, "Babylon Revisited," reminds us how poignant literary treatment of time can be.

A Question of Method

Some historians refer to the way they study the past as the historico-critical method. All three parts of this triple-barrelled phrase are important. "History" (or historico-) implies the awareness of the flux of time: things are always changing; the time one is studying is necessarily *different* from one's own. "Critical" is a word co-opted from the aspirations of the Enlightenment: in this phrase, it implies a baseline confidence in the capacities of reason to access and describe what really happened once one has overcome biases and prejudices. "Method" then follows naturally: the word encourages one to think of scientific ways of proceeding. With "method" one thinks of a certain kind of detachment, an attempt to isolate and control for x; one thinks of overcoming impediments to objectivity. Historicism, then, is indebted to rationality and even to rationalism. Such historicism does not radically accept the constraints of ideology and the limits of rationality of the sort to which theory draws attention.

New historicism is committed to a radical sense of the limits of rationality. It describes perspectivism in terms that it borrows from structuralism and deconstruction. For the literary critic, if "historicism" means thinking about the historical context in which a literary work is situated, the new historicist wants to overcome the text/context binary.

For the new historicist (as for the deconstructionist), *all we have is texts*. Meaning circulates between and among these various texts. One does not think of texts and contexts; one thinks of *co-texts*. For new historicists, "history is only available as a collection of discourses."[2] We're in a realm here very similar to Lacan's sliding chain of signifiers. We're in the realm of Saussurean linguistics!

We have already seen how Gadamer drew attention to preoccupation with method and with critical judgement as a foil to his radical approach to hermeneutics. There is overlap between new historicism and radical hermeneutics, to be sure. However, I would not place the latter under the umbrella of the former along with most other forms of contemporary theory. The reason is that, as we saw in the second section of this book, Gadamer, Ricoeur, and others defend rationality in ways that new historicists do not. New historicism owes more to deconstruction.

At issue in new historicism's description of history as a collection of discourses is the notion of a *unified* truth that might somehow motivate or vindicate the study of history. For this theory, there isn't one. The discourses can be collected in many different ways. One effect of this emphasis is that there can be no question of privileging one sort of text over another, whether in the name of "Literature" or any other label.[3] The upside is that one is encouraged to "study relations"[4] between texts. Such an approach encourages the finding of "patterns,"[5] especially those that reveal forms of power. The key point is that "*all texts* might be called interventions in such patterns."[6]

Furthermore, the turn to history entails that one can always question the meaning of a category at any given time. In new historicism, one term for this emphasis on ceaseless change and difference is one already encountered in previous chapters, "anti-essentialism." Rivkin and Ryan refer to "the anti-essentialism of the moment."[7] They do so not because they think anti-essentialism may be replaced by essentialism sometime down the line, but because they are conscious that even *that* term, anti-essentialism, is

---

2. Rivkin and Ryan, *Literary Theory*, 505/714.

3. Cf. Johnson's discussion of the problem of Literature with a capital L in the last chapter.

4. Rivkin and Ryan, *Literary Theory*, 506/714.

5. Rivkin and Ryan, *Literary Theory*, 506/714.

6. Rivkin and Ryan, *Literary Theory*, 506/715, emphasis mine.

7. Rivkin and Ryan, *Literary Theory*, 506/715.

serving as a category for the purposes of writing a meaningful sentence. They are implicitly aware that historicism eats away at the stability of any pronouncement whatsoever, even their own. They want (and need) to allow that anti-essentialism may look different sometime in the future. This is an issue to which we will return in the closing chapter.

Given the constraint of historicizing, words like "reality" often appear with qualifying quotation marks: ". . . show 'reality' to be constituted of systems of signs."[8] Any one version of reality is just that, a "version,"[9] with the inherent danger, *impossible* to avoid, of "occlusions."[10] The latter are deliberate or unconscious oversights of details of history that amount to exercises in silencing as a form of power. Who or what has been occluded in the study of history in the past? As we have already seen, women are good candidates, and so are minorities like indigenous people groups.

History and the Suspension of Unities

Michel Foucault is a key practitioner of new historicism. He brilliantly draws attention to the limitations of the way history is (or was) typically done. In "The Unities of Discourse," Foucault points out some of the ways historians create a sense of unity or meaning in the way they approach the past. In a long flourish, he lists four:

> But there is a negative work to be carried out first: we must rid ourselves of a whole mass of notions, each of which, in its own way, diversifies the theme of continuity. They may not have a very rigorous conceptual structure, but they have a very precise function. Take the notion of tradition: it is intended to give a special temporal status to a group of phenomena that are both successive and identical (or at least similar); it makes it possible to rethink the dispersion of history in the form of the same; it allows a reduction of the difference proper to every beginning, in order to pursue without discontinuity the endless search for the origin; tradition enables us to isolate the new against a background of permanence, and to transfer its merit to originality, to genius, to the decisions proper to individuals. Then there is the notion of influence, which provides a support of too magical a kind to be very amenable to analysis for the facts of transmission and

---

8. Rivkin and Ryan, *Literary Theory*, 507/715.
9. Rivkin and Ryan, *Literary Theory*, 507/715.
10. Rivkin and Ryan, *Literary Theory*, 507/715.

communication; which refers to an apparently causal process (but with neither rigorous delimitation nor theoretical definition) the phenomena of resemblance or repetition; which links, at a distance and through time as if through the mediation of a medium of propagation such defined unities as individuals, *oeuvres*, notions, or theories. There are the notions of development and evolution: they make it possible to group a succession of dispersed events, to link them to one and the same organizing principle, to subject them to the exemplary power of life (with its adaptations, its capacity for innovation, the incessant correlation of its different elements, its systems of assimilation and exchange), to discover, already at work in each beginning, a principle of coherence and the outline of a future unity, to master time through a perpetually reversible relation between an origin and an end that are never given, but are always at work. There is the notion of "spirit," which enables us to establish between the simultaneous or successive phenomena of a given period a community of meanings, symbolic links, an interplay of resemblance and reflexion, or which allows the sovereignty of collective consciousness to emerge as the principle of unity and explanation.[11]

Tradition, influence, evolution and development, "spirit": these four ways to establish continuity over time have dominated the study of history. Foucault's point isn't so much that unities don't exist; it's rather that they stop one from seeing other patterns. They occlude those other patterns.

The historian's typical unities give a sense of meaning that is rather like Lacan's Real. They're not as meaningful or truth-bearing as people think they are. Instead, they work in the way Nietzsche uncovers in his analysis of the word "serpent." If one recalls, that word captures some aspects of the reality of the beast at hand, but not others. The more basic reality than that captured by any continuity, Foucault insists, is "a population of dispersed events,"[12] that can be assembled in a variety of ways.

Foucault further reminds his readers that different terms to which historians appeal can themselves give the impression of capturing a unity that doesn't really exist. Such misrepresentation transpires in words like "literature" and "politics." Characteristics that one might think automatically belong to a category do not necessarily do so: "they are not intrinsic, autochthonous, and universally recognizable."[13] The word "universally"

11. Foucault, "Unities of Discourse," 90–91.
12. Foucault, "Unities of Discourse," 91.
13. Foucault, "Unities of Discourse," 91.

is noteworthy here. Dispersed events and historical artefacts are not accessible to a disembodied and universalized rationality. Fascinatingly, especially for students of literature, he points out that even the notion of a "book" isn't the unity that some people think it is!:

> There is the material individualization of the book, which occupies a determined space, which has an economic value, and which itself indicates, by a number of signs, the limits of its beginning and its end; and there is the establishment of an *oeuvre*, which we recognize and delimit by attributing a certain number of texts to an author. And yet as soon as one looks at the matter a little more closely the difficulties begin. The material unity of the book? Is this the same in the case of an anthology of poems, a collection of posthumous fragments, Desargues' Traite des Coniques, or a volume of Michelet's Histoire de France?[14]

Like the other theorists we have read, Foucault is very detail-oriented in his writing, with many specific insights and rich turns of phrase. He is among those theorists that Eagleton says engages in "scrupulously close reading."[15] Eagleton means to scold with this phrase, for some people mistakenly think of "close reading" as a traditional reading practice and quite distinct from what theorists do. Eagleton points out that this distinction doesn't hold. "The question is not how tenaciously you cling to the text, but what you are in search of when you do so," he goes on to say.[16]

Foucault is in search of a redescription of what passes as a rational exercise. He gathers the insights he presents to ask the question, what's the point of drawing attention to various unities *and then suspending them*? He supplies the following answer: "the systematic erasure of all given unities enables us first of all to restore to the statement the specificity of its occurrence."[17] Again, note the importance of a single word, this time "specificity." Foucault is after something very much like the specificity of Nietzsche's leaf. He wants the uniqueness of particular realities in all their irreplaceable uniqueness.

Foucault has two other points to make too. When we appreciate specificity, we can also perhaps see "other forms of regularity, other types

---

14. Foucault, "Unities of Discourse," 91.
15. Eagleton, *How to Read a Poem*, 2.
16. Eagleton, *How to Read a Poem*, 2.
17. Foucault, "Unities of Discourse," 93.

of relations."[18] The aim isn't to leave items alone in their specificity. Unities and patterns aren't in themselves bad. Rather, when one makes or sees other patterns (and this is a third point), one can do so in a way that is more self-aware. Foucault calls this a "controlled decision."[19] The emphasis falls on the interpreter, the pattern-maker. If Nietzsche draws attention to the truth-teller as a creator and an aesthete, so too Foucault identifies the historian as a creator.

The emphasis on what he calls "discursive formations" distinguishes Foucault from old-fashioned historicists. He both dissolves familiar unities and thinks in terms of language along Saussurean lines, in terms of its structure and arbitrary relations.

Culture, Context, and Co-Texts

Many readers, especially those who have had to buy literature textbooks, will have used a Norton anthology or a Norton critical edition. They're great texts! I have fond memories of starting my own collection when buying my first-year texts back in my hometown university. Norton is a very important publisher of English texts. They're also very traditional, a reliable brand. They're not the kind of company to go heavy into theory, especially in their introductory texts.

So it was a big deal when the company significantly altered a section on "Cultural and Historical Context" in the eighth edition of *The Norton Introduction to Literature,* a big, fat standard textbook. One might wish to point out that the word "context" remains in the section title. Strictly speaking, that doesn't sound like *new* historicism. It sounds like old historicism. To this astute observation, one might make two counterpoints. For one, it's still remarkable that Norton makes the changes it does at all; the alterations are a sign of the times. Secondly, despite the lingering presence of the word "context" in the title, when one looks at the section it feels like new historicism. There are lots of different texts *in circulation together* and there are important details that remind one of the importance of *language.*

The introduction in the eighth edition to the section "Cultural and Historical Context" runs to twenty paragraphs. As an interesting experiment, one might look at each of them for the following:

18. Foucault, "Unities of Discourse," 93.
19. Foucault, "Unities of Discourse," 94.

- Discussion of the literary text
- Discussion of context
- *Instances* of intertextuality (references to different texts)
- *Ideas* of negotiation, circulation, exchange
- An emphasis on language *per se*

The balance differs from paragraph to paragraph, of course, but in different ways a pattern emerges that shows the weight of new historicist considerations.

For instance, when one reads the first paragraph, one might notice the heavy emphasis on *language*:

> Over the past two hundred years, the meaning of the word *culture* has broadened considerably, from "enabling the growth of" (as in *agri*culture) to "the arts or familiarity with the arts" (*high* culture, a cultured *person*) to "a whole way of life" (*American* culture, *African American* culture). The fact that we still use the one word for both "the arts" and "a whole way of life" implies a close, even fundamental relationship between the two; it suggests that works of art reflect and help shape culture in the more comprehensive sense and also that art in a particular time and place takes the shape it does because of the larger cultural context—what nineteenth-century writer William Hazlitt called "the spirit of the age . . . ."[20]

The editors begin with a word study. Furthermore, the word studied is "culture"! That word allows for consideration of class, nation and race, aesthetics, and, by implication, specificity and difference. Attention is drawn to "a particular time and place." Right from the get-go, the editors immerse one in a new historicist approach. Admittedly, the reference to "'the spirit of the age'" involves an appeal to one of the unities that Foucault decries. To compensate, in the paragraphs that follow, the introduction takes pains to return to individual authors as well as their "cultural moment,"[21] specific times and places.

Another feature of the introduction is its incorporation—in practice—of numerous different co-texts. "Cultural and Historical Context" serves to introduce the story "Babylon Revisited," but it does more than that. It makes an interesting narrative in and of itself. The reader circulates

---

20. Beaty et al., *The Norton Introduction to Literature*, 490.
21. Beaty et al., *The Norton Introduction to Literature*, 490, emphasis mine.

between and slides from a dictionary set of definitions to another American story besides the one being introduced (written in roughly the same time period) to a critical study to biography to letters to the writings of a cultural critic writing in 1930 to a 1920s sociology text to a tract against prohibition to—last in my list, but definitely not least!—a series of *photographs*. Interspersed throughout the introduction, these latter items are *texts* in their own right, just as the wedding of Kate and William was. The photographs have their own contribution to make and need to be *read* appropriately. New historicism, and through it all theory, can take on added depth of meaning when one realizes experientially that it can help to open up what qualifies as a text.

Limits of Control in "Babylon Revisited"

As has been observed above, certain theories work especially well with certain texts. Why would the editors choose "Babylon Revisited" as the story to pair with new historicism as a reading strategy? One reason is that the story is about history! Charlie Wales has returned to Paris after the economic collapse of the late 1920s and that of his own life in alcoholism, the death of his wife, and the loss of his daughter to in-laws. He seems now to have his life under control and is seeking to gain custody of his daughter Honoria.

The title "Babylon Revisited" itself involves at least a twofold reference to history. The word "Babylon" recalls a city from ancient history and, specifically for Fitzgerald's audience, the Hebrew scriptures. The Babylonians once conquered the Israelites and took them into captivity. The Israelites wept for their native country "by the rivers of Babylon."[22] In part, the Israelite prophets disparaged Babylon as a city of decadence and irreverence, themes Fitzgerald invites the reader to associate with Paris and with the lifestyle of the Wales and their friends before the economic collapse at the end of the 1920s.

Secondly, the word "revisited" means to go back to some place or some time. The title actually carries with it a double going back, as if the reader were being invited to go back to a going back, as if one were being invited into an endless regress. One wonders if one can ever really know what happened in the past. The reader wonders what really happened between Charlie and his wife Helen, how much the dynamics with the in-laws contributed to what happened, what role the friends played.

22. Holy Bible, Psalm 137:1.

The story perpetuates open-endedness in the other direction too. The reader doesn't know what will happen beyond its ending. Readers want Charlie to be rewarded for his earnestness and hard work, yet the signs are ominous. Will Charlie ever get his daughter Honoria back? Everything seems right and he is working hard to be good, yet events conspire against him. At the end of the story, he has to wait six months before he can try again. We seem to be in the realm of Greek tragedy here. In the myth of Sisyphus, Sisyphus was condemned by the gods to roll a heavy rock to the top of a hill. Every time he did so, just before he reached his goal, he lost control of the rock and it rolled back to the bottom. The Greeks had a strong sense of fatalism.

In a way, Charlie has no one to blame but himself. At the very start of the story, he leaves the address of his in-laws Lincoln and Marion at the Ritz for "Mr Schaeffer" (580), a friend from the old days when they lived the high life together. His showing up with Lorraine Quarrles, another "of a crowd who had helped him make months into days in the lavish times of three years ago" (585) at exactly the wrong time seals Charlie's fate, at least for the time being. Duncan (Mr. Schaeffer) and Lorraine are described as ghosts: "Sudden ghosts out of the past" (585). Later, Lorraine, whose "passionate, provocative attraction" (585) Charlie still feels, sends him a *pneumatique*. A pneumatique is a kind of communication, like an email over a hardwired line, but in the form of a message in a tube. They were used in *Lost*. In North America, they are still used in places like Home Depot for sending data and cash from the cashiers to the offices. The word *pneumatique* contains the Greek word *pneuma*, which means spirit. Her message is a ghostly haunting. Other ghosts haunt Charlie too, especially the memory of his dead wife: "The image of Helen haunted him" (589). The whole world of Paris's fashionable and affluent Right Bank has a ghostly quality: "Outside, the fire-red, gas-blue, ghost-green signs shone smokily through the tranquil rain" (581). His relationship to this ghostly, haunting, and haunted environment is ambiguous. Charlie seems powerless to escape the past and to invite its influence.

When he leaves the Ritz for his in-laws, he has to cross "the logical Seine" (581): "Charlie felt the sudden provincial quality of the Left Bank" (581). A scant paragraph later, the reader is reminded of the feeling: "As they rolled on to the Left Bank, and he felt its sudden provincialism . . ." (581). Provincialism, from the perspective of someone who has enjoyed the high life, is a negative judgement, an indictment of the staid, bourgeois, logical, middle-class life of worry and resentment that Marion embodies. For Fitzgerald, a "Babylonian" lifestyle may have tragic implications, but crossing over the Jordan-like Seine to middle-class existence represents no kind of escape to or realization of a promised land.

Will Charlie get his daughter back? Will he have his deepest desire fulfilled? Will he achieve wholeness? When he meets Honoria, she flies to him, "struggling like a fish" (581). Can one ever catch a fish in one's arms? As a boy, if I ever tried to hold a fish in my arms, it would soon wriggle free and as likely as not fall into the water. Then there's the question of Charlie's drinking. I once knew an elderly woman who had a life-changing experience late in life that gave her liberty from her addiction, but she never touched alcohol again and never spoke of being a "former" alcoholic. Maybe Charlie never will get plastered again, like Lorraine and Duncan are in the climactic scene. Nonetheless, his elaborate efforts to control his drinking, like his rational, calculated efforts to control his environment, seem largely irrelevant in comparison with the larger forces at work in his world.

He wakes up one day happy and hopeful, but "suddenly" (590) he grows sad, just as he encountered "sudden provincialism" when he crossed the Seine. The past presses in on him at the very moment when he seems to have everything under control. Ancient Greek literature reminds us of human limitations. Fitzgerald reflects on such constraints in his contemporary context. It's not necessarily the case that humans lack meaningful freedom, but Fitzgerald's meditation on history readily aligns itself with postmodern theories of deferral, lack, and the dispersal of meaning.

Conclusion

New historicists share the concerns of many different theorists, from feminists and race theorists to deconstructionists. Like them, they privilege difference and particularities over the notion of universals or an objectively discernible truth. New historicism decries the unities to which historians sometimes unreflectively appeal to organize their investigations into the past. To the new historicist, the rational investigation of the past betrays a concern for unities that obscures the specificities and particularities of material reality. Such dispersed events confound the projects of an imposing, rational mind. The turn to language cements the philosophical critique of what seems rationally possible for the historian.

The student of literature, of culture, or of any number of other disciplines in the arts and social sciences, can apply new historicism since all their texts are historically situated. Not only does new historicism serve as an umbrella for many theories, it helps show the relevance of theory to many disciplines. It encourages the would-be theorist to pay ever more attention to registers of language and to what qualifies as a text.

Conclusion

Of Emperors and Little Boys

Terry Eagleton believes in the efficacy of collective action and the goal of economic equality, and he thinks that this political vision is being overwhelmed by the emphasis on arbitrariness and difference. Though an influential theorist in his own right, he argues against *some* ideas that pervade the discourse of literary theory. As such, he provides food for thought about the politics of theory and the different ways one might engage it.

Eagleton argues against the blunt application of an overriding idea like "difference." He takes a hard look at one of Nietzsche's driving ideas, a philosophical commitment later shared by Derrida and Foucault, and challenges it. We saw in an earlier chapter how Nietzsche talks about a leaf. In the following quotation, Eagleton returns to this leaf, but makes a different observation about it. In the context of mainstream theory, he sounds like the little boy commenting on the emperor's new clothes:

> Sanguine libertarians like Oscar Wilde dream of a future society in which everyone will be free to be their incomparable selves. For them, there can be no question of weighing and measuring individuals, any more than you could compare the concept of envy with a parrot.
>
> By contrast, pessimistic or shamefaced libertarians like Jacques Derrida and Michel Foucault see that norms are inescapable as soon as we open our mouths. The word "ketch," which as the reader will know means a two-masted fore-and-aft rigged sailing boat with a mizzen mast stepped forward of the rudder and smaller than its foremast, sounds precise enough, but it has to stretch to cover all sorts of individual crafts of this general kind, each with its own peculiarities. Language levels things down. It is normative all the way down. To say "leaf" implies that two incomparably different bits of

vegetable matter are one and the same. To say "here" homogenizes all sorts of richly diverse places.

Thinkers like Foucault and Derrida chafe against these equivalences, even if they accept them as unavoidable. They would like a world made entirely out of differences. Indeed, like their great mentor Nietzsche, they think the world *is* made entirely out of differences, but that we need to fashion identities in order to get by.[1]

Once again we see the presence of the artist in the midst of serious political and philosophical thinking. Oscar Wilde dramatized the desire to celebrate difference. Eagleton presents Wilde's conviction that "there can be no question of weighing and measuring individuals" in a detached way, but he probably agrees wholeheartedly.

Nonetheless, our linguistic reality poses an unavoidable challenge to the celebration of uniqueness: "Jacques Derrida and Michel Foucault see that norms are inescapable as soon as we open our mouths." Norms are rules that impose themselves upon our reality. However much one may wish to celebrate difference, when we use language we do something that complicates that simple desire. Eagleton's first illustration of this fact—his reference to a "ketch"—may leave the reader bewildered, but shame on us if we don't spot the allusion in the second! "To say 'leaf,'" he writes, "implies that two incomparably different bits of vegetable matter are one and the same." He is of course referring to Nietzsche's essay "On Truth and Lying in the Extra-Moral Sense." When one expresses oneself as a linguistic creature and at the same time holds to difference as a guiding idea, one is caught in a contradiction. To recognize the contradiction is to have a twinge of misgiving. As Eagleton puts it, Foucault and Derrida acknowledge that we "fashion identities in order to get by." The notion of "getting by" is an admission that something doesn't quite work satisfactorily. It's like putting a band-aid on a cut to a lifeline.

Eagleton may not accuse Nietzsche, Derrida, and Foucault of inconsistency, but he does make clear the limitations of emphasizing only difference in language:

> It is true that nobody in a world of pure differences would be able to say anything intelligible—that there could be no poetry, road signs, love letters or log sheets, as well as no statements that everything is uniquely different from everything else.[2]

1. Eagleton, *After Theory*, 14.
2. Eagleton, *After Theory*, 14–15.

CONCLUSION

In this book, I have tried to show that mainstream theory tends in this direction of "a world of pure differences." We have seen that the editors of a major anthology of theory not only describe but endorse the position that "Ideas and things are like signs in language; there are no identities, only differences," and that "This idea challenged the central assumptions of metaphysics."[3] They prioritize difference and leave one alone to confront the—strictly speaking—impossibility Eagleton points out.

As the famous theorist goes on to say in a very witty paragraph, we simply don't behave as if there were only differences, and when we insist on such a slogan we behave like abstract idealists.[4] This is the case even though the right and proper insistence on the value of material reality bars the way to abstract idealism. Difference has become a guiding idea.

In his own fashion, Eagleton has tried to be the little boy in the story of the emperor's new clothes. He has tried to point out an obvious lack. Yet, having written these words almost twenty years ago, he can hardly be said to have succeeded in dispelling the emperor's embarrassment or in having set the kingdom to rights.

Post-Critical Hope

Theory, like literature itself, exposes glib assumptions about rationality. As an impetus to reflect on the nature and claims of rationality in human experience, theory is of inestimable value. It has become integral to the study not only of literature but of all arts disciplines. At the same time, it seems that Nietzschean nihilism and Derridean deconstruction give the theorist an acid that can eat away at any text, any belief, any hope. Theory can easily reduce to a set of slogans, jargon, name-dropping, and unconsidered ideas. Despite the rightness of the critique, this study has also suggested that, in mainstream theory, one finds oneself at the court of an emperor with no clothes on. There are obvious reasons for feeling uncomfortable, a discomfort that doesn't have to do only with unfamiliar jargon and names.

Two options present themselves to the fledgling theorist. One can either join in unmasking rationality and explicitly seeking to undermine it, or one can seek a renewed understanding of what rationality itself might be. The redescription of our cultural endeavours in terms of power and violence, heterogeneity and difference, affords powerful and necessary correctives,

3. Rivkin and Ryan, *Literary Theory* 2, 258.
4. Eagleton, *After Theory*, 15.

but remains incomplete. In the latter case, the project may depend on one's revising their understanding of the nature of reality. For all the problems and paradoxes associated with it, rationality remains inalienable to human flourishing. It remains integral to the nature of the arts and of politics. To the extent that theory illumines art, it cannot afford to turn on rationality altogether. The same is true of its relevance to our political discourse.

Rationality has an often reduced meaning in modernity or in a scientific understanding of reality. It has a role to play in arts and social science disciplines beyond that. Within a view of reality as participatory, it remains central, and with it confidence in language. Both have the power to encourage an awareness of transcendent mystery at the heart of reality that invites our whole-person, embodied, and assenting response. Mystery accompanies rationality at every stage of its operations. In literature and philosophy, in science and in art, reason is forever entwining with something other that shapes what it itself must be. No self-contained conception of it can satisfy the deepest desires of the human heart, yet every step along the way it can encourage in us those yearnings and foster the hope of their fulfilment.

If rationality can do that, though, it simultaneously reveals failures. We fail to follow where it leads. On a personal, a social, and a systemic level, we find a strange process at work so that the best of what we plan and do can somehow work against us. In correspondence with the author, Eagleton observed that "one needs of course in Marxian mode to be properly dialectical about the Enlightenment, like bourgeois history itself both a delight and a disaster." As we have seen, rationality signals at once an ability to surpass ourselves (enabling the development of culture) and the propensity to *hubris*. Greek tragedy and Christian original sin attest personal responsibility. They also announce limitations so perplexing they seem built into that with which rationality has to do, or at least naturalized to it, irreducible to personal culpability. On all levels, we seem unable to live in what seems to be an appropriate call to continual responsiveness to that which lies at the heart of creation. The idea of doing so exhausts us.

Yet wherever we encounter reality (or, better: wherever we become aware of reality as "belonging-to")—which literature and art can help us so often to do—hope is renewed. Perhaps this happens best in the moments when we also confront limits in ourselves and our ability to control the world around us. We can cunningly misconstrue this hope as a renewed determination to conquer. Hope as genuine hope, though, presents itself to us from the outside. It encourages us in ways entirely in accord with our personal being as rational and desiring creatures: we appear made to flourish. Yet it also pulls us up and out of ourselves. This seems to be rationality's destiny.

Bibliography

This book introduces key ideas and its running theme through a series of very short readings and excerpts. A number of these have been anthologized by Michael Rivkin and Julie Ryan in *Literary Theory: An Anthology* (Blackwell, as of 2017 in its 3rd edition). References to readings from this text are given, where possible, in the form 765/894 to capture the pagination in both the second (2004) and third (2017) editions (in that order). In the bibliography below, the page ranges in both editions are also supplied where applicable; the rest of the entry provides the information for the third edition. Where the text appears in only one of these two editions, that edition is noted as part of its short title, e.g., *Literary Theory* 2. This text includes editorial introductions to each of the theories and readings to be discussed, and these introductions are treated in the same way. References to poems and short stories are generally given in the form of references to anthologies. Some of these are readily available online.

Atwood, Margaret. "Bluebeard's Egg." In *The Riverside Anthology of Short Fiction: Convention and Innovation*, edited by Dean Baldwin, 1039–58. Boston: Houghton Mifflin, 1998.
Avison, Margaret. "The Hid, Here." *Always Now: The Collected Poems*, vol. 2. Erin, ON: Porcupine's Quill, 2004.
Barfield, Owen. *Saving the Appearances: A Study in Idolatry*. 2nd ed. Middletown, CT: Wesleyan University Press, 1988.
Barrett, William. *Irrational Man: A Study in Existentialist Philosophy*. New York: Doubleday, 1958.
Beaty, Jerome, et al. "Cultural and Historical Context." In *The Norton Introduction to Literature,* 8th ed., edited by Jerome Beaty et al., 490–98. New York: Norton, 2002.
Carpenter, Humphrey. *J. R. R. Tolkien: A Biography*. London: Grafton, 1992.
Dante Alighieri. *Paradiso*. Edited and translated by Courtney Langdon. Cambridge: Harvard University Press, 1921.

BIBLIOGRAPHY

Dennett, Daniel. *Darwin's Dangerous Idea: Evolution and the Meanings of Life.* New York: Simon and Schuster, 1995.

Derrida, Jacques. "Différance." Rivkin and Ryan, 278–99/474–81.

Eagleton, Terry. *After Theory.* New York: Basic, 2003.

———. *How to Read a Poem.* Oxford: Blackwell, 2007.

Fink, Bruce. *Lacan to the Letter: Reading* Écrits *Closely.* Minneapolis: University of Minnesota Press, 2004.

Fitzgerald, F. Scott. "Babylon Revisited." In *The Riverside Anthology of Short Fiction: Convention and Innovation,* edited by Dean Baldwin, 579–94. Boston: Houghton Mifflin, 1998.

Foucault, Michel. "Unities of Discourse." In *Literary Theory: An Anthology,* 2nd ed., edited by Julie Rivkin and Michael Ryan, 90–94. Oxford: Wiley Blackwell, 2004.

Freud, Sigmund. "The Uncanny." Rivkin and Ryan, 418–30/592–614.

Gadamer, Hans-Georg. "The Universality of the Hermeneutical Problem" (1966). In *Philosophical Hermeneutics,* translated by David E. Linge, 3–17. Berkeley: University of California Press, 1976.

Grant, George. *English-Speaking Justice.* 1974. Reprint, Toronto: Anansi, 1998.

Heaney, Seamus. "Eclogues *in Extremis*: On the Staying Power of Pastoral." *Proceedings of the Royal Irish Academy* 103C (2003) 1–12.

———. "The Outlaw." In *The Norton Introduction to Literature,* 7th ed., edited by Jerome Beaty and J. Paul Hunter, 657. New York: Norton, 1998.

Henry, Michel. *La barbarie.* 1987. Reprint, Vendôme: PUF Quadrige, 2001.

Herbert, George. "The Windows." *The Longman Anthology of British Literature,* 4th ed., edited by David Damrosch and Kevin J.H. Dettmar, 1632–33. New York: Longman, 2010.

Hofstadter, Douglas R. *Gödel, Escher, Bach: An Eternal Golden Braid.* 1979. Reprint, New York: Vintage, 1980.

The Holy Bible. NRSV. Grand Rapids: Zondervan, 1989.

Irigaray, Luce. "The Power of Discourse and the Subordination of the Feminine." *Literary Theory: An Anthology,* 2nd ed., edited by Julie Rivkin and Michael Ryan, 795–98. Oxford: Blackwell, 2004.

Johnson, Barbara. "Writing." Rivkin and Ryan, 340–47/528–35.

Kant, Immanuel. "What Is 'Enlightenment'?" Translated by Mary C. Smith. http://www.columbia.edu/acis/ets/CCREAD/etscc/kant.html.

Kearney, Richard. *On Stories.* London: Routledge, 2001.

Kumin, Maxine. "Woodchucks." In *The Norton Introduction to Literature,* 7th ed., edited by Jerome Beaty and J. Paul Hunter, 628. New York: Norton, 1998.

Lacan, Jacques. *Écrits: The First Complete Edition in English.* Translated by Bruce Fink et al. New York: Norton, 2005.

———. "The Mirror Stage as Formative of the Function of the I as Revealed in Psychoanalytic Experience." Rivkin and Ryan, 441–46/618–23.

———. "Seminar on 'The Purloined Letter.'" *Écrits,* translated by Jeffrey Mehlman. *Yale French Studies* 48 (1972). https://www.lacan.com/purloined.htm.

Langland, William. *Piers Plowman: A new annotated edition of the C-text,* edited by Derek Pearsall. Exeter: University of Exeter Press, 2008.

Linge, Alfonso. "Editor's Introduction." Gadamer, xi–lviii.

Lowe, Lisa. "Heterogeneity, Hybridity, Multiplicity: Marking Asian American Differences." In *Literary Theory: An Anthology,* 2nd ed., edited by Julie Rivkin and Michael Ryan, 1031–35. Oxford: Blackwell, 2004.

Macmurray, John. *Reason and Emotion.* 1935. Reprint, London: Faber and Faber, 1995.

Mannheim, Karl. *Ideology and Utopia: An Introduction to the Sociology of Knowledge.* New York: Harcourt Brace, 1949.

Murdoch, Iris. "Above the Gods." In *Existentialists and Mystics: Writings on Philosophy and Literature,* 496–531. London: Chatto and Windus, 1997.

Myers, Jack. *The Portable Poetry Workshop.* Portland: Ringgold, 2004.

Nietzsche, Friedrich. "On Truth and Lying in an Extra-Moral Sense." In *Literary Theory: An Anthology,* 2nd ed., edited by Julie Rivkin and Michael Ryan, 262–65. Oxford: Blackwell, 2004.

Olds, Sharon. "Sex without Love." In *The Norton Introduction to Literature,* 7th ed., edited by Jerome Beaty and J. Paul Hunter, 934–35. New York: Norton, 1998.

Penny, Steven. "Breaking Bad: 'What about the soul?'" YouTube, https://www.youtube.com/watch?v=a-Qva8lG4mY

Pieper, Josef. *The Silence of St Thomas.* Translated by John Murray and Daniel O'Connor. South Bend, IN: St Augustine's, 1999.

Poe, Edgar Allen. "The Purloined Letter." http://xroads.virginia.edu/~Hyper/POE/purloine.html.

Ricoeur, Paul. "Toward a Hermeneutic of the Idea of Revelation." In *Essays on Biblical Interpretation,* edited by Lewis S. Mudge, 73–118. Philadelphia: Fortress, 1980.

Rivkin, Julie, and Michael Ryan, eds. *Literary Theory: An Anthology,* 3rd ed. Oxford: Wiley Blackwell, 2017.

Rorty, Richard. "Remarks on Deconstruction and Pragmatism." *Deconstruction and Pragmatism,* edited by Chantal Mouffe, 13–18. London: Routledge, 1996.

Safranski, Rüdiger. *Nietzsche: A Philosophical Biography.* Translated by Shelley Frisch. New York: Norton, 2002.

De Saussure, Ferdinand. *Course in General Linguistics.* Rivkin and Ryan, 59–71/138–74.

Sprat, Thomas. *A History of the Royal Society, for the Improving of Natural Knowledge.* London: F. Martyn, 1667.

Suzuki, David. "Environmentalism and the Responsibility of Academia." *Academic Matters* April-May (2008) 5–8.

Timmons, Vianne. "Equal Opportunities Bring Excellent Outcomes: A Response to Margaret Wente." *University Affairs,* 17 November 2017. https://www.universityaffairs.ca/opinion/in-my-opinion/equal-opportunities-bring-excellent-outcomes-response-margaret-wente/.

Williams, Rowan. "The Archbishop of Canterbury on the Royal Wedding." YouTube https://www.youtube.com/watch?v=-8msHZ8wI7Y.

———. *Grace and Necessity: Reflections on Art and Love.* London: Continuum, 2005.

Williams, William Carlos. "The Use of Force." https://web.stanford.edu/dept/HPS/force.html.

Index

aesthetic, aesthetics, 25, 44, 76–77, 139
After Theory, 27, 71–73, 145–46
alienation, 74, 76–78, 81
Anglo-American, 6, 34–36, 44, 60
arbitrariness, 31, 96, 109, 111–13, 120, 144
Aristotle, 6, 73, 86, 115
Asian-American, 36–40, 42–43
Atwood, Margaret, 30–33, 37
Avison, Margaret, 89

"Babylon Revisited," 133, 139–40
Bacon, Francis, 104
Barfield, Owen, 55n23
"Bluebeard's Egg," 30–33, 37, 62
border, 37, 96
bourgeois, xiv, 111, 127, 141, 147
Breaking Bad, 45–46
bureaucracy, bureaucratic, bureaucratization, xiv, 2, 16

canon, 25, 31, 46
Catholic, 48
Chang, Diana, 40–41
Chaucer, Geoffrey, 25, 79
Chicano, 36–37
child, childish, 20, 43, 55, 58, 95
childhood, 54, 122, 130
Christ, Jesus Christ 48
Christendom, Christian, Christianity, 48–49, 104, 115, 127, 147
cogito, ergo sum, 49–50, 104, 125
constructivism, 26–27, 37

Course in General Linguistics, A, 100, 103, 107–13, 121, 123
critical race theory, xiii, 6, 35–37, 42, 44, 48, 60–62, 66, 100, 101, 132

Dante Alighieri, 92–93
Darwin's Dangerous Idea, 8
deconstruction, xiii, 113–14, 118–21, 127, 132–34, 142, 146
Dennett, Daniel, 8
Derrida, Jacques, 101, 103, 107, 109, 113–19, 120–21, 127, 144–45
Descartes, René, 47–50, 78, 104, 111, 125
différance, 117
difference, 101, 106, 109, 112–15, 117–18, 120, 125, 132, 134–35, 139, 142–46
double, 51, 53–55, 110, 140
dream 48, 50–52, 121, 123–25
Durkheim, Émile, 55n23

Eagleton, Terry, 68, 70–74, 77, 82, 84–85, 103, 118, 137, 144–47
economic, economics, xiv, 1–2, 111, 137, 140, 144
Eliot, T. S., 87, 89
emperor's new clothes, 3–4, 144, 146
Enlightenment, 19, 47, 67, 78, 101, 103–4, 133, 147
essentialism, essentialist, essentialize, 25–27, 39–40, 42, 50, 134–35

feminism(s), xiii, 6, 23–28, 33, 37, 42, 60–61, 66, 99

INDEX

finitude, 62, 66
Fitzgerald, F. Scott, 133, 140–42
Foucault, Michel, 133, 135–39, 144–45
Freud, Sigmund, 6, 45, 47–48, 50–56, 59, 61–62, 65, 100–101, 106, 120–23, 125, 131

Gadamer, Hans-Georg, 68, 74–79, 81–82, 85, 87, 134
Galileo, 104
Gödel, Escher, Bach: An Eternal Golden Braid, 81n1
Grace and Necessity, 87–89
gynocriticism, 25, 31

Handmaid's Tale, The, 30
Heaney, Seamus, 8–9, 16–18
hegemony, 35–36, 42, 54
heimlich, 55
Herbert, George, 90–92
hermeneutics, 74–75, 77–78, 81–87, 89, 96, 134
"Heterogeneity, Hybridity, Multiplicity: Marking Asian American Differences," 34, 38–43, 66, 93, 100–101, 132
"Hid, Here, The," 89–90
historico-critical method, 133
Hoffmann, E. T. A., 52–53
Hofstadter, Douglas, 81n1
hubris, 6, 66–67, 81, 147

ideology, 60–61, 65, 133
in medias res, 5–6
Inside Out, 49, 51
Interpretation of Dreams, The, 48, 52, 121
"Introduction: Introductory Deconstruction," 114
Irigaray, Luce, 25–29, 33, 38, 42, 54

jamming the machinery, 33
Jentsch, Ernst, 52–54
Johnson, Barbara, 110–11, 123–24, 126–28, 134n3
Joyce, James, 25
judgement, 36, 68–80 (esp. 74–78), 81, 134

Kant, Immanuel, 101n5
Kate, HRH Princess, 93–94, 140
Kearney, Richard, 86–87
Kumin, Maxine, 16, 18

Lacan, Jacques, 100–101, 120–25, 128, 130, 131, 132, 134, 136
lack, 120, 122, 130, 142
Langland, William, viii, 4, 8
Latino, 36–37
Lévi-Strauss, Claude, 107–8, 121
Lévy-Bruhl, Lucien, 55n23
Lewis, C. S., 99, 107
limitation, 1–2, 6–7, 18, 26, 36, 46, 62, 66, 69, 73, 117, 119, 131, 135, 142, 147
Literature, 127, 134
Louis XIV, 31
Lowe, Lisa, 34–35, 37–44, 54, 66, 100, 132
Luther, Martin, 48

Macmurray, John, 68–71, 73–74, 77, 79, 82, 85, 89
Mannheim, Karl, 60
Marx, Marxian, Marxist, 71, 110–11, 132, 147
McDonald's, 15
Meditations on First Philosophy, 47, 49
method, 1, 5, 8, 46, 73, 75, 83, 107, 133–34
mimic, mimicry, 27–31, 33, 48, 54
mimesis, 29, 86–87
modern, modernism, modernity, 1–2, 7, 47–49, 55, 59, 66–68, 70, 73–75, 77–78, 80, 83–85, 88, 103–4, 109, 116, 147
Monopoly, 30
moreness, xiv, 89
Myers, Jack, 13–15, 82
mystery, xiv, 7–8, 91, 93–94, 96, 147

Native American, 36–37
Nazi, 19
Nietzsche, Friedrich, 7, 77, 100–101, 103–7, 120, 126–27, 133, 136–38, 144–46

154

INDEX

new criticism, 99n1, 108, 121
new historicism, 132–35, 138, 140, 142–43
nihilism, nihilistic, 20, 104, 146
Norton Introduction to Literature, The, 133, 138–39

Oedipus, 52–53, 66
Olds, Sharon, 16, 19, 21
"On Truth and Lying in an Extra-Moral Sense," 104, 145
oral, orality, 31, 33, 36–37, 44, 118
Orthodox, 48
oeuvre, 136–37
"Outlaw, The," 16–18, 82

participation, 85–86, 89–96, 111–12
Perrault, Charles, 31
Pieper, Josef, 7n7
Plato, xiii, 6, 79–80, 90, 115–17, 119, 120
Poe, Edgar Allen, 120, 128–29, 131
poetics, 82–87
Portable Poetry Workshop, The, 13–15
postmodern, postmodernism, xiii, 72, 114, 118, 142
post-structuralism, 104, 114–15, 120–21
power, xiii, 3–4, 19, 22, 26, 27, 37–44, 58, 61, 69, 101, 105, 120, 134–35, 146
"Power of Discourse and the Subordination of the Feminine, The," 27–29
prejudice, 74, 78, 133
Protestant Reformation, 48–49
psychoanalysis, 6, 45, 47–52, 53, 59, 61, 66, 100–101
"Purloined Letter, The," 120, 128–30

radical hermeneutics, 74, 81, 134
Rank, Otto, 54
rationalism, xiv, 133
Real, the, 120, 132, 136
Reason and Emotion, 69–71, 89
rebus, 123–25, 131
referent, referentiality, 110, 112
referential function, 83–86, 102
religion, 49, 101, 127
representation, 18, 39, 85, 127, 136

repression, 22, 45–59, 105, 119, 121, 123, 132
Rich, Adrienne, 25
Ricoeur, Paul, 81–89, 96, 102, 134
Rivkin, Julie and Michael Ryan, 2–3, 24–27, 34–37, 45, 50–52, 66, 99–100, 104, 108–9, 113–16, 121–22, 132, 134–35, 146, 149
Rockwell, Norman, 56, 86, 95
Rorty, Richard, 118, 127–28
royal wedding, 93–94
Russian formalism, 108, 121

de Saussure, Ferdinand, 100–101, 103, 107–15, 120–21, 123, 125, 131, 133–34, 138
Schleiermacher, Friedrich, 77–78
science, 1–2, 5–6, 14–15, 45–46, 49, 51, 66, 74–75, 83–85, 101–2, 104, 109, 127, 147
Seneca, 128
"Sex without Love," 16, 19–20
Shakespeare, William, 15, 84, 123–24, 125n10, 131n17
sign, signified, signifier, xiv, 14, 94, 108–13, 115, 117, 123–26, 130, 134–35, 137, 141, 145–46
signifying chain, 123–24, 130
Silence of St Thomas, The, 7n7
social science, xiii–xiv, 1, 4, 99, 143, 147
Socrates, 78–79, 115–17
Sprat, Thomas, 102, 108–9, 112–13, 122
Strand, Mark, 14–15
structuralism, 100, 107–10, 114–15, 120, 121, 133
Suzuki, David, 1–2

Tan, Amy, 35, 43–44
Tolkien, J. R. R., 99, 107
tragedy, tragic, 32, 66, 141–42, 147
"Two Kinds," 35, 43–44

"Universality of the Hermeneutical Problem, The," 74
University Affairs, 65
"Uncanny, The," 52–55, 82
uncanny, uncanniness, 51–55

155

INDEX

"Use of Force, The," 56–58, 62, 95

violence, 17–18, 39, 49–50, 56, 58, 67, 96,
    100, 107, 120, 130, 146

Wilde, Oscar, 144–45
William, HRH Prince, 93–94
Williams, Rowan, 81, 87–89, 94
Williams, William Carlos, 56–58
"Windows, The," 90–91
"Woodchucks," 16, 18–19
"Writing," 110, 111n21, 123–27